Judge this book by its cover!

Curiosity about the title, the current information security landscape, creation of an information security program, a need for your business, word of mouth, professional career development, or just personal growth—any one of these could be the reason why you are contemplating the purchase of this book, or you have already bought it and are now wondering whether you invested wisely. I would like to think that you will be pleased after having read it. This book is in fact the best book in the marketplace pertinent to building highly secure software, but you don't have to take my word for it.

The famous adage goes, "Don't judge a book by its cover" but for once, I think that saying does not hold true. When it comes to this book, "*The 7 Qualities of Highly Secure Software*," you can judge this book by its cover. And, as you read between the covers, you will realize that your decision to invest in it was not only worthwhile but certainly wise.

Below are some quotes/testimonials from a diverse sampling of business professionals who had the opportunity to read the book and provide their feedback.

–Mano Paul

*"This will be **required reading for my executives, security team, software architects and lead developers**. Paul continues to set the pace for software assurance leaders."*

David W. Stender, CISSP, CSSLP, CAP
CISO, U.S. Internal Revenue Service

*"One thing I have learned over the years is you don't need to be a security expert to improve the security of your systems. **You only need to know some core, critical skills to raise the security bar on the attackers to swing the game in your favor.** Mano Paul's* The 7 Qualities of Highly Secure Software *will help you achieve that goal by teaching you significant and much-needed skills."*

Michael Howard
Principal Cybersecurity Architect, Microsoft
Author, *Writing Secure Code*

*"With the increasing trend of businesses to leverage virtual (cloud) and mobile environments, **developing highly secure software should be at the forefront of organizational strategy and this book provides a framework to do so**. Written in a style that is easy to understand, Paul identifies the 7 qualities of highly secure software that must be factored into any software development project. Regardless of whether your role is business- or technology-centric, this book is a must-have if your goal is to build, deploy, and maintain reliable and resilient software."*

Troy Leach
CTO, PCI Security Standards Council

*"While some software development companies have begun to actively consider security in their design, the vast majority of organizations in their systems integration and various development activities often do not have any form of programmatic approach to this topic. **This important book and the approach it outlines should be required reading for organizations.** Mano has translated his experience and knowledge into a very approachable book on a key topic and I highly recommend this book."*

David Melnick, CISSP, CISA, CIPP
Security, Privacy and Data Protection Division, Deloitte & Touche LLP
Board Member, (ISC)²

*"The foremost expert on secure software development, Paul has written a book that incorporates a gripping storytelling style to **focus on the SDLC principles needed to build hacker-resilient software**. His clever use of illustrations, metaphors, family anecdotes, and childhood stories brings the key lessons or 'qualities' critical to building highly secure software to life."*

Pat Myers, CISSP-ISSMP, CRISC
ISSA Distinguished Fellow

THE 7 QUALITIES OF

🔒 7

HIGHLY SECURE
SOFTWARE

THE 7 QUALITIES OF

HIGHLY SECURE
SOFTWARE

Mano Paul

CRC Press
Taylor & Francis Group
Boca Raton   London   New York

CRC Press is an imprint of the
Taylor & Francis Group, an **Informa** business
AN AUERBACH BOOK

CRC Press
Taylor & Francis Group
6000 Broken Sound Parkway NW, Suite 300
Boca Raton, FL 33487-2742

© 2012 by Taylor & Francis Group, LLC
CRC Press is an imprint of Taylor & Francis Group, an Informa business

No claim to original U.S. Government works

Printed in the United States of America on acid-free paper
Version Date: 20120417

International Standard Book Number: 978-1-4398-1446-8 (Hardback)

Visit the Taylor & Francis Web site at
http://www.taylorandfrancis.com

and the CRC Press Web site at
http://www.crcpress.com

Contents

Preface xi

About the Author xv

1   **Quality #1: Security Is Built In, Not Bolted On** 1
    Prelude: The Ant and the Grasshopper 1
    Introduction 2
    Security Myths That Need Busting 3
        Myth #1: We Have a Firewall 4
        Myth #2: We Use SSL 8
        Myth #3: We Have Intrusion Detection Systems
        and Intrusion Prevention Systems (IDSs/IPSs) 12
        Myth #4: Our Software Will Not Be Accessible
        from the Internet 14
        Myth #5: We Have Never Been Compromised 15
        Myth #6: Security Is "Not My Job" but the
        Responsibility of the Service Provider 16
        Myth #7: Security Adds Little to No Value to the
        Business 18
    Build Security In: The Need 20
    Build Security In: What It Takes 24
    Build Security In: The Value-Add 27
    Conclusion 28
    References 29

2 Quality #2: Functionality Maps to a Security Plan **33**
Prelude: Breaking the Tape 33
Introduction...34
What Is a Security Plan? 35
Security Plan Development..................................38
    Step 1: Identify Security Objectives............................39
    Step 2: Identify Applicable Requirements 40
    Step 3: Identify Threats...40
    Step 4: Identify Applicable Controls.........................40
Benefits of a Security Plan..................................42
Mapped Software 44
Conclusion..46
References 47

3 Quality #3: Includes Foundational Assurance Elements **49**
Prelude: What Lies Beneath?...............................49
Introduction...50
Data: The New Frontier 51
Data under Siege..53
Foundational Assurance Elements.......................54
    Confidentiality 54
    Integrity 58
    Availability 62
    Authentication...64
    Authorization 66
    Auditing 68
Conclusion..70
References 71

4 Quality #4: Is Balanced **73**
Prelude: The Clown Fish and the Anemone.......73
Introduction...74
Balancing Scale: Risk and Reward 74
Balancing Scale: Functionality and Assurance.....77
Balancing Scale: Threats and Controls................80

Conclusion 82
References 86

**5 Quality #5: Incorporates Security
Requirements 87**
Prelude: Lost in Translation 87
Introduction.. 88
Types of Software Security Requirements 89
Techniques to Elicit Software Security Requirements 95
Traceability of Software Security Requirements 99
Requirements to Retirement 99
Conclusion...100
References 101

6 Quality #6: Is Developed Collaboratively 103
Prelude: There Is No "I" in Team! 103
Introduction..104
Stakeholders in the Game: Whose Perspective? 105
  Business 106
  Security 106
  Management 107
  Development 110
  Legal.. 110
  Privacy 112
  Auditors.. 113
  Vendors.. 114
Conclusion.. 116
References 117

7 Quality #7: Is Adaptable 119
Prelude: The Shark is a Polyphyodont........................... 119
Introduction..120
Law of Resiliency Degradation.......................................120
Software Adaptability: Technology, Threats, and Talent 122
  Technology 122
  Threats 125
  Talent 127

Begin with the Future in Mind...129
Secure Software Requires Security-Savvy People...........130
Conclusion..131
References 131

8 Epilogue..133

Index.. 135

Preface

Internationally recognized, respected leadership authority, family expert, teacher, and renowned author, Dr. Stephen Covey is no stranger to those in the business world. His #1 bestseller, *The 7 Habits of Highly Effective People,* is rightfully recognized as one of the most influential business books of the twentieth century with more than twenty million copies sold in thirty-eight languages.

I wondered what it would be like if I met Dr. Covey and asked him to write a book on software security that is prevalent or emerging today. Interestingly, what I believe he would write is that there is a striking parallel between *The 7 Habits of Highly Effective People* and *The 7 Qualities of Highly Secure Software.*

Using anecdotes and analogies from Aesop's fables, athletics, architecture, biology, nursery rhymes, video games, etc., I have attempted to take what would otherwise be deemed complex and dry and highlighted the qualities of highly secure software in an informative and interesting way. This book is about the seven qualities of highly secure software; and once you understand what these qualities are, you will notice that those who design, develop, and deploy highly secure software are also highly effective in their personal and professional lives. Each chapter in this book describes one of the seven highly secure software qualities, and the synopsis of each chapter is given here.

Quality #1: Security Is Built In, Not Bolted On

Habit #1 of highly effective people is to "Be Proactive." Quality #1 of highly secure software is that security controls are built in from the initial stages of its design, through development to deployment, and not bolted on at a later stage in the software development life cycle (SDLC). The cost of fixing software defects (including security defects) discovered after it has been released is estimated to be significantly greater than if discovered earlier in the SDLC. This chapter starts out by dispelling common security myths and covers the reasons and value of being proactive; incorporating security from the initial phases of your SDLC, instead of bolting it on at a later phase.

Quality #2: Functionality Maps to a Security Plan

Habit #2 of highly effective people is to "Begin with the End in Mind." Quality #2 of highly secure software is that the functionality of the software maps to a security plan. This means that a plan needs to exist in the first place, a plan not just for the functionality of your software but one for security as well. This chapter covers the elements of an effective security plan for software, beginning with the end in mind, and also covers the mechanisms to construct and track your software security controls on how they map to the plan.

Quality #3: Includes Foundational Assurance Elements

Habit #3 of highly effective people is to "Put First Things First." Quality #3 of highly secure software is that your software includes certain foundational elements of protection. This means that the software is built on a strong foundation and is secure by design, in development, and in deployment. This chapter covers putting first things first; addressing the foundational assurance elements of confidentiality, integrity, availability, authentication, authorization, and auditing; and the importance of data protection.

Quality #4: Is Balanced

Habit #4 of highly effective people is to "Think Win–Win." Quality #4 of highly secure software is that it is balanced: balancing risks and investment to return, functionality with assurance, threats with controls. This chapter explores what it takes to create a win–win situation with a balanced approach to security in the software being designed, developed, and deployed.

Quality #5: Incorporates Security Requirements

Habit #5 of highly effective people is to "Seek First to Understand, Then to Be Understood." Quality #5 of highly secure software is that it incorporates security requirements adequately. Requirements may be externally imposed or internally mandated, and regulatory, private, or compliant in nature. This chapter starts by covering the types of requirements that need to be incorporated into the software from a security perspective and then discusses different techniques to elicit security requirements from these sources. It ends by discussing the importance of tracking these requirements as an effective step to seek first to understand and then to be understood.

Quality #6: Is Developed Collaboratively

Habit #6 of highly effective people is to "Synergize." Quality #6 of highly secure software is that it is collaboratively developed. It is important to take into account the perspectives of the different stakeholders. These stakeholders include the client, security, management, development, legal, privacy team, auditors, and vendors as well. Development team members can act as liaisons to the security organization. This chapter discusses the need for synergy between the various stakeholders as they collaborate in building highly secure software.

Quality #7: Is Adaptable

Habit #7 of highly effective people is to "Sharpen the Saw." Quality #7 of highly secure software is that it is adaptable: adaptable to changing technologies, threats, and the talent pool. This means that the software's ability to withstand attack is continuously being improved to ensure that software developed today is secure not only after its release but that it is designed to address new and emerging threats. This chapter starts out by describing the law of resiliency degradation and then discusses what software adaptability is. It concludes by highlighting the fact that secure software requires security-savvy people and highlights the importance of awareness, training, and education to keep the saw sharpened.

I trust that this book will be useful in your efforts to help your company build highly secure software. I hope you enjoy reading this book as much as I enjoyed writing it.

Mano Paul
CSSLP, CISSP, AMBCI, MCAD,
MCSD, CompTIA Network+, ECSA

About the Author

 **Manoranjan (Mano) Paul** is the software assurance advisor for (ISC)², the global leader in information security education and certification, representing and advising the organization on software assurance strategy, training, education, and certification. He is also a member of the Application Security Advisory Board. He is the winner of the inaugural Information Security Leadership Awards (ISLA) as a practitioner in the Americas region. His information security and software assurance experience includes designing and developing security programs from compliance-to-coding, security in the SDLC, writing secure code, risk management, security strategy, and security awareness training and education.

Paul started his career as a shark researcher in the Bimini Biological Field Station, Bahamas. His educational pursuit took him to the University of Oklahoma where he received his degree in business administration in management information systems (MIS) with various accolades and a coveted 4.0 GPA. Following his entrepreneurial acumen, he founded and serves as the CEO and president of Express Certifications, a professional certification assessment and training company that developed studISCope, (ISC)²'s official self-assessment offering for their certifications. Express

Certifications is also the self-assessment testing company behind the U.S. Department of Defense certification education program as mandated by the 8570.1 Directive. He also founded SecuRisk Solutions, a company that specializes in security product development and consulting. Before Express Certifications and SecuRisk Solutions, Paul played several roles from software developer, quality assurance engineer, logistics manager, technical architect, IT strategist, and security engineer/program manager/strategist at Dell, Inc.

Paul is the author of the *Official Guide to the CSSLP* (Certified Secure Software Lifecycle Professional) and is a contributing author to the *Information Security Management Handbook*, and has contributed security-related material several times to the Microsoft Solutions Developer Network (MSDN). He has served as vice president, industry representative, and an appointed faculty member of the Capitol of Texas Information System Security Association (ISSA) chapter and vice president of the Cloud Security Alliance (CSA), Austin Chapter. He has been featured at various domestic and international security conferences and is an invited speaker and panelist, delivering talks, training, and keynotes at conferences such as the SANS, OWASP, ASIS, CSI, Gartner Catalyst, and SC World Congress. Paul holds the following professional certifications: CSSLP, CISSP, AMBCI, MCSD, MCAD, CompTIA Network+, and ECSA certification.

Paul is married to the most wonderful and self-sacrificing person in this world, Sangeetha Johnson, and their greatest fulfillment comes from spending time with their sons, Reuben A. Paul and Ittai A. Paul.

Chapter 1

Quality #1: Security Is Built In, Not Bolted On

Go to the ant, thou sluggard; consider her ways, and
be wise: which having no guide, overseer, or ruler,
provideth her meat in the summer, and gathereth her
food in the harvest.

—*Proverbs 6:6*

Prelude: The Ant and the Grasshopper

As a child, one of my favorite activities was to have my dad
read and tell us the stories from Aesop's fables. One story that
left an indelible imprint in my mind is the story of the ant and
the grasshopper. You may be familiar with this story, but for
the benefit of those who are not, the story goes something
like this.

In a field one summer's day, a grasshopper was hopping
about, chirping and singing to its heart's content. An ant
passed by, bearing along with great toil an ear of corn he was
taking to the nest. "Why not come and chat with me," said the

grasshopper, "instead of toiling and moiling in that way?" "I am helping to lay up food for the winter," said the ant, "and recommend you to do the same." "Why bother about winter?" said the grasshopper; "we have got plenty of food at present." But the ant went on its way and continued its toil. When winter came, the grasshopper had no food and found itself dying of hunger, while it saw the ants distributing every day corn and grain from the stores they had collected in the summer. Then the grasshopper knew: It is best to prepare for the days of necessity.

In a similar manner, when it comes to secure software, it is best to prepare for the days ahead. One must be proactive to infuse necessary security processes and controls throughout the software development life cycle and not just before software gets released or deployed, to make the likelihood of a successful hacker attack impossible or next to impossible.

Introduction

Quality #1 of highly secure software is that security is built into the software from the initial stages of its design, through development to deployment, versus being bolted on at a later stage in the software development life cycle (SDLC). However, because incorporation of security features can potentially take more time and cost the project more, arguments challenging the adoption of, or opposing the need for this quality can be raised by someone who is required to incorporate security from the get-go.

Challenges and opposition often take the form of questions or comments such as, "Why do I really need to take security into account when my organization is already hard-pressed for time to deliver the software to the customer?"; "Adding on nonfunctional features such as security controls hardly seems to add any business value to my project."; "Incorporating security in the development life cycle is not only risky for my project, as it can result in the slipping of its deliverable date, but it is also going to be costly as I have to pay for the personnel resources needed."; or "I don't see the benefits of doing additional work at a cost when I don't know for certain if the software we develop will even get hacked." None of these questions or comments are invalid from a business perspective, and so they must not be ignored or viewed solely from a security vantage point.

Such opposition does not always come from the business users or project managers alone. Even from within the Information Technology (IT) organization, some have argued, "We already have a firewall, and we use Secure Sockets Layer (SSL) for secure transmission, so why do we need more security in our software?"; "Shouldn't the networking and security team take care of protecting our company?"; or "Our Intrusion Detection Systems (IDSs) and Intrusion Prevention Systems (IPSs) should detect and prevent attacks against our company, correct?"

In essence, all these challenges to the adoption of secure software life-cycle processes and opposition to incorporate security controls from the start of a project are, in fact, attempting to answer this one question: What is the value-add for being proactive in building security into the software we develop?

Security Myths That Need Busting

Before we delve into answering the value proposition question, we must first recognize that some of these challenges are actually misconceptions that must be set correct. These are myths that need to be dispelled.

If we were to approach Jamie Hyneman and Adam Savage, the stars of the Discovery channel's show called *Mythbusters*, and ask them about the most common software security-related myths that are common and prevalent today, it is highly likely that upon their research, they would compile a list similar to the one below.

1. We have a firewall.
2. We use SSL.
3. We have intrusion detection systems and intrusion prevent systems (IDSs/IPSs).
4. Our software will not be accessible from the Internet.
5. We have never been compromised.
6. Security is "Not my Job" but the responsibility of the service provider.
7. Security adds little to no value to the business.

Let's take some time to dispel these myths.

Myth #1: We Have a Firewall

Arguably, this is one of the most common arguments posed when it comes to incorporating security throughout the software development life cycle. Unfortunately, this is a remnant of an infrastructure security *modus operandi* and is extremely myopic. It often stems from the way companies have implemented security historically. In earlier days, there was clear demarcation between a company's boundary and the outside world, and the role of a security professional was primarily network defense configuration and operations. For the most part, when people talked about a security professional, they were talking about a network security professional such as a firewall administrator.

I can still remember, in my early days of information security work, one of the clients I worked for was trying to build their application security program, but instead of finding the right talent to develop the program, they had chosen to move some of the network security professionals, who were familiar with firewall administration, into the application security group as consultants. The network architecture manager was also inappropriately appointed as the acting information security officer, and very soon it was noticeable that every solution that these network security professionals recommended for application security concerns was to implement a firewall. The repercussion this had was that the development team members not only had very little say in incorporating security into the software they designed, but they also started to become complacent about security, pushing it off as a network or infrastructure problem. These network security professionals had clearly not understood the application security domain and were providing incorrect guidance that created a placebo sense of security.

Another incident comes to mind: I was invited to be a panelist on application security at an information security conference and when asked about the trends in the arena of information security, I made the statement that the "Era of the network hacker is fading!" to express the fact that the types of attacks that are evident today are targeted at applications or software. I received an email from a person in the crowd telling me that I did not know what I was talking about. Upon further discussions with this individual, it was quickly apparent to me that he was, by profession, a network security firewall administrator. He and his manager had attended the talk and the issue that he was trying to address was not necessarily the veracity of my statement, but rather his personal job security. If his manager had taken my statement to be more than what was intended, it could potentially be misconstrued as a threat to this individual's job. But the fact that can be substantiated from research findings is that more and more companies are falling prey to attacks that exploit weaknesses in software (applications). Gartner Group, in 2005, published that approximately 70 percent of attacks were targeted at the application layer.

The argument that we must be secure because we have a firewall in place is not only weak, but also misleading. In today's computing environment, not only has the boundary that defined a company's borders thinned out, but in certain situations this boundary is practically nonexistent. Take, for example, the trend that is evident in many organizations to leverage cloud computing. Here platforms, infrastructures, and software are consumed using an on-demand, pay-per-use subscription model. Companies purchase a subscription to the services provided by the software and not the software itself. Furthermore, depending on the type of cloud computing implementation, such as private/public or hybrid clouds, company data may not be housed within the boundaries of the company itself. In implementations where company data is housed externally in the cloud provider's infrastructure, as in the case of a public cloud, your company's firewall offers no protection at all.

Vanishing Boundaries

In today's computing environment, not only has the boundary that defined a company's borders thinned out, but in certain situations this boundary is practically nonexistent, thus requiring the need for secure software!

Additionally network firewalls provide no protection against attacks that originate from within the company. This group of attacks is perpetrated by individuals who are within the company or who have access to the internal systems of a company *viz.* the insiders. A disgruntled employee or someone who a competitor could have planted within your company are examples of threat agents who are insiders. Developers who defect and implant logic bombs in code, which is now part of the attack surface, also fit this profile. Sadly, the network firewall can do little to protect against the enemies inside the firewall.

The Enemy Inside the Firewall

Network firewalls provide no protection against attacks that originate from within the company.

Perimeter defense controls such as network firewalls have their place in software security as one of the first lines of defense. They are certainly necessary, but they cannot be the only control to protect internal applications. For example, firewalls are usually effective for *ingress* filtering of maliciously crafted packets, but when it comes to *egress* filtering, it is recommended that firewalls are used in conjunction with data loss (or leakage) prevention (DLP) technologies. They are useful in protecting against network flooding and denial-of-service (DoS) attacks but provide little to no defense against data theft and data-related attacks.

If you still have not bought into the fact that firewalls on their own are inadequate to provide the assurance of security that is necessary, let me assert this with a simple illustration. If you take a hammer and smash an egg, the outer shell will crack. The mess that is left behind is directly proportional to whether the egg was boiled (hardened) or not. In cases where the egg is not boiled, a big mess results, and the yolk (the nutritious part) of the egg spills out. On the other hand, if the egg is boiled, little to no mess occurs, even when the shell cracks. Now liken the eggshell to that of a network firewall and the internal yolk to the data of your company, which is your most valuable asset—second only to the people resources within your company. Boiling the egg is analogous to hardening your internal systems and applications so that even when there is a break in the network defenses (eggshell), the internal assets are not compromised (spilled out). Figure 1.1 shows a picture of a cracked eggshell and the payload that could exploit the vulnerability represented in binary shellcode format. The eggshell is certainly necessary but the inside of the egg needed to be hardened as well. Hardening the egg can be achieved by systematically incorporating security into the software development life cycle. This is akin to not just relying on the lock on your door, but placing your jewels within a locked safe inside your home.

Myth #2: We Use SSL

Second only to the "We have a firewall to make us secure" myth is the misconception that "We use SSL and so we must be secure."

Figure 1.1   Boiling the egg is analogous to hardening your internal systems and applications so that even when there is a break in the network defenses (eggshell), the internal assets are not compromised (spilled out).

Before delving into dispelling this myth, we must first understand what SSL is and how it works. SSL, which stands for Secure Sockets Layer, is a protocol that protects data transmission by creating a secure tunnel between a browser and the Web server hosting the Web application, as the name indicates. Data that is transmitted in this secure channel is protected because it is encrypted by the SSL certificate, which is issued after the company's identity is verified by a certificate authority (CA). It provides certificate-based authentication and protects against man-in-the-middle (MITM) attacks. What happens under the covers is a five-step process as illustrated in Figure 1.2.

First, the browser requests the identity information of the Web server. The Web server responds by providing its SSL certificate to prove its identity. The browser then checks to see if the SSL certificate presented is one that can be trusted or not, meaning it is not part of the revoked certificate list. If it trusts the presented SSL certificate, it sends a message back to the Web server indicating that it trusts the Web server. The Web server now sends an acknowledgment that is digitally signed so that the client and the Web server can now start a secure tunnel for communication. An SSL encryption session is started, and data that are shared between the browser and the Web server are encrypted.

Rewind to the late 1990s, just about the time that the Internet was gaining dominance, the special report in the

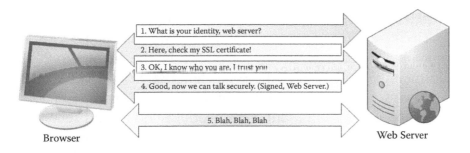

Figure 1.2   Secure Sockets Layer (SSL): How it works.

Electronic Business magazine entitled "Dangers without, Dangers within: Network security in the age of e-commerce" reported the arrest of Carlos Felipe Salgado, Jr. (who called himself "Smak") by the Federal Bureau of Investigation (FBI). "Smak" was charged with five counts of violating Title 18, United States Code, Section 1030(a)(4) for having hacked and accessed protected computers used in interstate and foreign commerce and communication without authorization, and by means of such conduct, obtained credit card numbers with a combined credit limit in excess of $1 billion. "Smak" was arrested in a sting operation led by the FBI's special agent Dalrymple, at the San Francisco International Airport, where he had agreed to meet and sell 100,000 stolen credit card numbers for $260,000 to a cooperating witness of the FBI, whom he believed was a customer. Richard Power and Rik Farrow, in their writeup "Are you ready for Electronic Commerce Crime?," highlight that the websites that Salgado hacked by exploiting known operating system vulnerabilities and placing sniffers were indeed protected using firewalls and SSL, but he had gotten around them.

Now fast-forward to a little over ten years since the arrest of Carlos Felipe Salgado, Jr. If you attended the Blackhat USA conference in 2009, you would have had the opportunity to hear Moxie Marlinspike, a security researcher, talk and demonstrate tricks to defeat SSL using open source tools called sslsniff and sslstrip that he developed. These tools leverage an MITM attack methodology combined with spoofing and HyperText Transport Protocol (HTTP) stripping attacks.

These attacks are evidence of the fact that SSL is not foolproof; but if you are still not convinced, let me attempt to illustrate the limitation in the protection that SSL provides by borrowing an illustration from Vittorio Bertocci, who uses a clothes metaphor to describe the need for end-to-end security and not solely rely on the opaqueness of the environment. In his analogy, he presents three scenarios, as depicted in Figure 1.3.

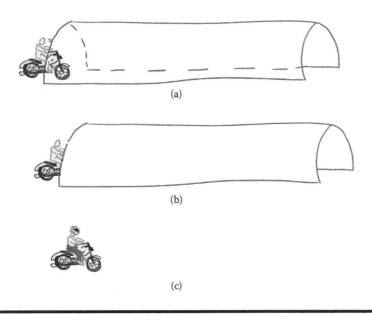

Figure 1.3 Why you shouldn't drive your motorcycle naked? Source http://blogs.msdn.com/b/vbertocci.

In scenario (a), a naked motorist goes through a transparent tunnel. This is analogous to unprotected data being transmitted on a nonsecure channel (such as HTTP). The data is susceptible to attack from its point of origin to its destination and even when it is being transmitted.

In scenario (b), the naked motorist goes through a tunnel that is opaque. This is analogous to unprotected data being transmitted on a secure channel (such as one protected by SSL; HTTPS). As long as the data is in transit (on the wire), it is protected, but there is no assurance that the data is protected from its point of origin until it enters the tunnel or while the data is at rest (in storage).

In scenario (c), the motorist is clothed and does not rely on the opaqueness of the environment. This is analogous to the data being protected by some means, such as encryption and/ or hashing, and whether it is transmitted over a secure or a nonsecure channel, it is less susceptible to disclosure, even if captured.

SSL is a necessary security control to protect data in transit, but it does not necessarily protect applications against all threats. SQL Injection and Cross-Site Scripting (XSS) attacks, which make the one-two punch attacks against Web applications today, are both possible, even when SSL is enabled on the Web server. Additionally, researchers Juliano Rizzo and Thai Duong have shown that Browser Exploits Against SSL/TLS (BEAST) undermines SSL protection by abusing a vulnerability that is present in major Web browsers, which allows an adversary to efficiently decrypt and obtain authentication tokens and cookies from HTTPS requests.

Myth #3: We Have Intrusion Detection Systems and Intrusion Prevention Systems (IDSs/IPSs)

The deployment of IDSs/IPSs to detect and prevent attacks is less than optimal in providing assurance if the information collected by these systems is not monitored and acted upon. Most IDS/IPS systems collect a plethora of information that ranges from simple innocuous alerts to incidents that are truly malicious. The sheer amount of information collected can be overwhelming to anyone tasked with the manual inspection of threats. Real threats can be buried in voluminous datasets of IDS logs. Not acting on, or not having the ability to act on, the information collected by the detection sensors is like having a treadmill at home but not using it, but yet expecting to be fit.

Because a comprehensive inspection of IDS/IPS log data manually is nearly an impossible task, as these technologies have matured, we have resorted to automated correlations of events to threats or threat agents. Such automation requires the pre-definition of threat signatures to be used as a blacklist or the recording of normal behavior to detect anomalies.

The degree of assurance provided by pattern matching IDS/IPS is directly proportional to the correlation abilities of the IDS/IPS, in conjunction with the appropriate implementation of the blacklist and the training of the security operations personnel tasked to monitor these logs. Blacklist filters can be bypassed by canonicalization attacks. Canonicalization is the mechanism by which an alternate representation of data resolves to a standard (or canonical) form. So when an attacker passes in an alternate representation of the pattern being matched, the blacklist filter can be bypassed. When the security decision is made based on noncanonical forms, then the software must be architecturally robust in handling input appropriately. When noncanonical representations are observed in the logs, the monitoring personnel should be trained to identify and raise a "red flag" to spur further research and investigation. For example, if one notices in their IDS logs an entry that has the following text, %u00ABscript%u00BB, then they must be trained to recognize that this is a Unicode representation of the word <script> as the characters %u00AB get canonicalized to the left angle bracket (<) and the characters %u00BB get canonicalized to the right angle bracket (>). Further research needs to be done immediately to verify if there is an attempt to evade Cross-Site Scripting (XSS) filters, or not.

Bypassing Blacklist Filters

Blacklist filters can be bypassed by canonicalization attacks.

Additionally, the monitoring engine must be configured to identify software security patterns to make correct correlations to threat. For example, if the following, "SELECT first_name, last_name, email FROM CUSTOMER where user_name = 'sjohnson' WAITFOR DELAY '0:0:10,'" is captured in the IDS log files, then the correlation engine should be configured to alert on WAITFOR DELAY signatures and the monitoring personnel must be trained to recognize that WAITFOR DELAY statements can lead to any of the possible outcomes: sql injection, race conditions, or denial-of-service (DoS). Normalization of logs to eliminate duplicates and synchronize time, along with visualization (plotting) of the log data are useful for discerning patterns and behavior.

While an IDS is primarily reactive in nature, an IPS is proactive. Just as both the "Check Engine" and "Airbag" functionalities are required for the automobile to pass safety requirements, both IDSs and IPSs are required for a company to ensure a reasonable degree of assurance. But the premise that "We have host and network IDSs (HIDS and NIDS) and IPSs and so we must be secure" is like saying that the safety of the car is solely dependent on the "Check Engine" and "Airbag" functionalities. These technologies must be deployed, complementing other defense in-depth measures such as perimeter defense controls, malware protection on the hosts, and hardened applications.

Myth #4: Our Software Will Not Be Accessible from the Internet

It is no surprise that the most secure computer is the one that is not connected and turned on, another myth that is prevalent in companies is that they must be secure because their internal software and applications are not accessible by external users. While this may be the case in companies that primarily develop software for commercial or internal use, it does not mean that they are necessarily secure, because this myth does not take into account the *insider* threat profile.

This misconception is not a recent development that has come about because of the increase in connected technologies, but harks back to the 1980s. The article "Security Myths" that was published in the *Supergroup* magazine in July 1988 had as Myth #6, "My users are too dumb to do anything nasty." Recent statistical data paints the picture that the percentage of external threats to internal threats is more or less leveled and shares equitable percentages, vacillating around the midpoint. Actually, it is not the ranking of how many threats were initiated from the outside versus the inside that is important. The extent of damage that can be caused is a more serious consideration that cannot be ignored.

Just as a person takes into account both external and internal factors to stay fit, companies should pay attention to both the external threat agents and the insiders, and assuming that they are secure because of the restriction or lack of connectivity from the outside world is akin to not ignoring the medical recommendations from the travel safety clinic regarding food and weather that are external factors when traveling abroad, but completely ignoring maladies that can lead to a gangrenous situation.

Myth #5: We Have Never Been Compromised

The "Security Myths" article published in the *Supergroup* magazine lists that the most pernicious myth of all is: "It only happens to the other guy." Unfortunately, this is still a very prevalent notion in many companies today, who argue that we must be secure because we have never been compromised. This is evident from the ten immutable laws of security administration, a Microsoft TechNet publication that lists "Nobody believes anything bad can happen to them, until it does" as Law #1. Unfortunately, when a security breach occurs and when "the shit hits the fan" (pardon the language), it is a big mess left behind, and a realization dawns on the victims that they now agree with the Thirteenth-century English jurist Henry de Bracton that "an ounce of prevention is worth a pound of cure."

To those who continue to take the stand on this myth that we will wait and see if it (a security breach) could happen to us, I often tell them about William Shakespeare's play, "The Tragedy of Julius Caesar" and the scene in which Julius Caesar meets a soothsayer on his way to the Theatre of Pompey, where he will be assassinated. In that meeting, the soothsayer foretells of the harm that will befall Caesar and warns Caesar to beware the Ides of March. Caesar ignores that warning, branding the soothsayer as a dreamer and tells him, "The Ides of March are come," to which the soothsayer responds, "Ay, Caesar; but not gone." Later Caesar is assassinated, as the soothsayer had warned him.

Beware, The Ides of March

Julius Caesar: The ides of March are come.
Soothsayer: Ay, Caesar, but not gone.

I am not an advocate of promoting security using fear, uncertainty, and doubt (FUD), for I would much rather manage a security program using measurable data and metrics. But sometimes the only way to motivate people to take security into serious consideration, especially if they, believe that they will not be compromised because they it has not happened previously, is to paint the picture that branding those who seek the protection for your company as dreamers can have nightmarish consequences.

Myth #6: Security Is "Not My Job" but the Responsibility of the Service Provider

One of the games that I play when I have time is poker (with poker money of course, because gambling is unwise). Poker gained popularity in the mid-nineteenth century in the United States. In the interest of fairness, to address concerns of players who were suspicious of cheating and dirty dealers, the right to deal a hand was rotated among the players. The dealer was given a token marker. This was usually a knife with a handle that was made of a buck's horn and, in short, referred to as a buck or button. When a hand was over, the individual who was next in line to deal would be given the buck. Later, silver dollars were used in place of the buck horn knife as a marker and is most likely the reason why the term "buck" is used as a slang for the dollar. The phrase "passing the buck," which has become a metaphor to dodge responsibility by passing it off to someone else or blame someone else, is known to have its origin in the game of poker.

As companies have adopted recent trends of as-a-service computing, prevalent in cloud computing, be it Infrastructure as a Service (IaaS), Platform as a Service (PaaS), or Software as a Service (SaaS), a myth that security responsibilities can be passed to the service provider has unfortunately become a side effect. The "Security of Cloud Computing Provider" publication, however, reported contrary expectations by the service provider. The salient points in the report not only mention that the majority of cloud providers did not consider security a competitive advantage to them but alarmingly reflect that the cloud providers felt that securing the cloud was the responsibility of their customers and not their own. From this it is evident that both the customer and the provider seem to be passing the "security buck" to the other. In reality, security in shared hosting solutions should be a shared responsibility. The report also indicated that cloud computing providers allocate 10 percent or less of their operational resources to security. Such low allocation of operational resources to security is unwise.

Having a "security is not my job" mindset and relying on the service provider to secure your systems and applications is a hand that you cannot bet on; and if you do, a hacker may call your bluff and guess what? You are busted.

President Harry Truman used the phrase, "The buck stops here" to signify that one must be willing to accept one's responsibilities. Both the customer and the service provider must be willing to accept their responsibilities for security. While the provider takes into account infrastructure- and platform-based security measures, the customer should focus on building applications with security built in to run in the cloud. The onus is more on you as a customer to ensure that security is implemented in the infrastructure, platform, and applications because when a breach occurs, your customers are going to look for someone to blame. Guess what, it will not be the hackers or the service provider.

Myth #7: Security Adds Little to No Value to the Business

The paradox of value is an economic theory that is attributed to Adam Smith, who in his work, "An Inquiry into the Nature and Causes of the Wealth of Nations," observes that goods that are useful for life (e.g., water) are less valuable in exchange, for water would buy scarcely anything or be exchanged for anything while other goods that have little use for existence (e.g., diamonds) are highly valuable in exchange. This is also referred to as the diamond–water paradox, and the laws of supply and demand govern this paradox. Because water supply is considerably more than the supply of natural diamonds, its value is not as substantial. Having said that, the demand for these goods must also be factored in. An individual in a desert who is dying of thirst would not hesitate for even a second to give away his valuable diamonds for a glass of water.

The myth that security adds little to no value to business functionality can also be viewed from the paradox of value perspective. Although security is useful for the very existence of the company, it seems like it cannot really buy as much in return as would business functionality that can create wealth. When business functionality contends with security functionality, it is obvious that the former trumps the latter. However, we must not only take into account the "value in use" and "value in exchange" aspect of the paradox of value when determining the value of information security, but must also consider the need (demand) for security. For a company that has been breached, security becomes a vital consideration to survive— as opposed to a company that has not been breached.

The Paradox of Value in Security

One must take into account the "Value in Use," "Value in Exchange," and the "Demand for Security" when determining the value-add of security.

The myth that security adds little to no value to business can be attributed to many reasons, two of which are discussed here. The first is that the definition of value is myopic, and the second is that not there is no clear understanding of value as it pertains to return and savings.

The myopic definition of value has its roots in viewing the value of software purely from a customer perspective, wherein value is defined as useful and usable functionality that is delivered to the customer. Because security functionality is often implemented under the covers, and is not visible to the customer as functionality (unless the requirements explicitly state it, which is not usually the case), its value is perceived as significantly less than that of business functionality. But perception is not the same as reality, as security adds value in terms of enabling the business to continue operations to generate expected business value. For example, if your e-commerce store is susceptible to a Cross-Site Scripting (XSS) attack that leads to a denial-of-service attack that defaces your e-commerce store website, then the business cannot continue and loses more in terms of time (downtime) and revenue. Developing the e-commerce software to protect against XSS attacks in a sense enables the business to continue its operations and generate the expected business value via sales.

Second, the value of security should not be purely viewed from a return-on-investment vantage point, but also from a savings perspective. Although the return on security investment (ROSI) may not be directly observable in terms of revenue generation, the value that security brings to the business in terms of *cost savings* is substantial, some of which cannot even be quantified. Return is about wealth creation while savings is about wealth preservation, as Richard Bejtlich writes in the TaoSecurity blog. We must be cognizant of the difference between the two and recognize that while security is generally a cost, not creating money, it saves money. It saves money in terms of time to fix vulnerabilities. Not only is there monetary benefit brought about by cost savings, but *brand savings* that is brought about by security in the software is of far greater significance. Keeping the company name out of the front-page news as a victim of a security breach is invaluable, because reputational damage can be irreparable.

So this notion that security adds little to no value to the business is an erroneous misconception that only the uninformed tout, despite the fact that it is a moot point.

Build Security In: The Need

Full disclosure security lists and vulnerability databases are testaments to the fact that the software applications developed in our companies today are insecure. Reported incidents in the chronology of data breaches, published by Privacy Rights Clearinghouse since 2005, indicate that over 535 million sensitive data records have been exposed as a result of more than 2,000 attacks. Over 310 million of the 535 million data records were breached as a result of hacking, and a little over 30 million records were disclosed as a result of insiders going rogue. Interestingly, the list of reported companies that were victims of a security breach did not only include some small businesses, but also some medium to large enterprises. The industries represented by these victims ranged from businesses, to retail, military, government, financial, insurance, medical, educational, and even non-profit organizations. If the attacks seemed to target only small businesses, often characterized by an *ad hoc* software development methodology, then one can conclude that these attacks are possible due to weaknesses in processes; but because these attacks have plagued large businesses such as Sony and even RSA, which are expected to have a software development methodology in place, the problems may not be just process related, but people and technology related as well. One needs to holistically address security in software, which is twofold in approach: one is to look at the people, process, and technology aspects of software security and the other is to look at the assurance capabilities of the software as it interplays with other hosts in and out of the company network.

With an annual cost of $180 million or more attributed to insecure software, as reported in the acclaimed book titled *Geekonomics*, by author David Rice, the problems that stem from insecure software are not something insignificant. Cost savings alone is a motivator for having the need to develop highly secure software, but not all motivations can have a price tag tied to it. For example, the reputational damage and loss of customers that result when a company is breached have significant repercussions pertaining to the continuity of the business itself. Companies such as Sony, from which more than 100 million user accounts and passwords were stolen by a series of hacks would incur colossal monetary damages, estimated to be in billions (not millions) of dollars, but even that would be deemed diminutive in light of the loss of brand and faith in the company that their customers had.

Additionally, the landscape of security is evolving. With the move toward globalization, outsourcing and offshoring have gained a lot of traction in today's business world. The software that is deployed may be developed by a team of developers who are not under your direct control, and such situations have greater potential for insider threats, such as the implantation of logic bombs and backdoors in code. Globalization has also had an effect on the boundaries that define a company. These boundaries are slowly vanishing and in some cases indistinguishable. When the perimeter thins, there is a heightened impetus to secure the internal assets of the company by building security into the software that is developed. Current-day trends of subscription-and-service-based computing (e.g., cloud) models have increased this vanishing perimeter problem, as the perimeter in some cloud computing delivery models (e.g., public clouds) is practically nonexistent.

The security landscape has also changed in regard to the motivation of hackers. In my earlier days of work in security, the attacks against organizations were for the most part nonintrusive and motivated by a "cool" ego factor. It was cool to be the kid on the block who could deface a website or do a DoS attack. For the most part, no irreparable damage was done, other than disruptions and denial-of-service that led to a frustrated victim. Nowadays, however, the ballgame is different; and while defenders have to play by a new set of rules, attackers have the advantage of not having to play by these rules. Current motivations of hackers are of far greater consequence to the victims because attacks are motivated not just from a "cool" factor, but from a "cash" factor and/or "cause" factor. Phishing and social engineering attacks that aim to circumvent any disclosure protection that is in place can fetch a lot of money (cash) by the sale of confidential or sensitive information (such as Personally Identifiable Information or credit card numbers). "The Cybercrime Service Economy" article published in the *Harvard Business Review* starts out by stating that criminal hacking has spawned a full-blown service economy that supports the preponderance of script kiddies but fulsomely larcenous hackers. It further reports that cybercriminal services entrepreneurs who are willing to take the risk of apprehension, prosecution, and incarceration continue to pursue their interests because the cash benefits, which amount to millions of dollars each month, significantly outweigh the risks. In addition to cash being a motivator, some newer trends indicate that "cause" is another motivator in this changing security landscape. The April 2011 issue of *The Hacker News,* titled the "Anonymous edition," listed the series of attacks performed by the Anonymous hacking group and the reasons for most of these attacks. These reasons ranged from supporting the freedom to express a personal or political agenda to responding against legal and censorship of fellow hackers. The #OpSony attacks of the Anonymous group against Sony was a retaliation against Sony's pursuit to sue George Hotz (GeoHot) and Alexander Egorenkov (Graf_Chokolo), who had hacked the Sony PlayStation3, as depicted in Figure 1.4.

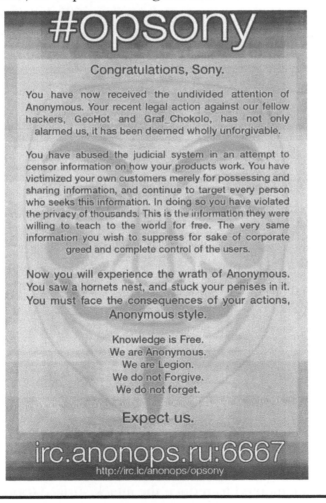

Figure 1.4   Anonymous' reason for hacking Sony.

Lulzsec, which is another hacker group, has demonstrated similar motivations, as has Anonymous. They were brought to International attention after they hacked the American Public Broadcasting Service (PBS) and stole user data. They claimed that this attack was motivated to defend WikiLeaks and Bradley Manning, an American Army soldier who was arrested in Iraq for having leaked sensitive information to the WikiLeaks website. Anonymous and Lulzsec are examples of hacker groups that are motivated by cause: to express their opinions freely on what they deem is not right in relation to freedom of expression and individual privacy. An understanding of hacker motivation is essential to understand the reason for the cybercrime.

The 3 Cs that Motivate Hackers

Hacker motivations range from being "cool" to "cash" and "cause," and it is important to recognize the driving forces behind cybercrime.

Furthermore, the attack targets have moved from networks and hosts to applications. Lulzsec used an SQL injection attack against Sony. The Distributed DoS (DDoS) tool RefRef, purported to be developed by Anonymous, leverages JavaScript and vulnerabilities within SQL to create a DoS against the targeted website. This warrants a new kind of defender profile, one that understands how software works and what it takes to break or exploit software so that they can defend against these software attacks.

Build Security In: What It Takes

Of the three elements necessary to perpetrate any crime—*viz.*, motive, opportunity, and means—unfortunately there is not a lot that can be done to address motive, but security controls can be implemented to reduce the attack surface (opportunities) and means by which a hacker might compromise your software. Security controls are of two types: proactive (safeguards) and reactive (countermeasures).

Building security in is about proactively designing and developing appropriate security controls into the software. The quality of building security in that will result in highly secure software can be achieved by addressing the people, the process, and the technology components in the software engineering process.

The results of the Forrester Forrsights Security Survey published in *Application Security: 2011 and Beyond* indicates that application security is viewed as a priority, but investment still remains tentative. It highlights that changing the attitude toward application security would require a shift in organizational behavior that will create a culture that places importance on *proactive* risk management rather than immediate return on investment (ROI).

Such a shift requires strategic planning and long-term commitments, and this begins with the people. Unfortunately, the fallacy in most security programs today is a tool-centric approach to addressing application security concerns.

We need to make strategic investments in application security and not just tactical tool-based solutions. Let me try to explain with an illustration that hits home. Every year, for about 3 years in a row, my wife and I would find ourselves at the onset of summer in our backyard pulling weeds from our lawn using a weed-removal tool known as the weed hog. Not only was this an energy-consuming effort, but it would also take us more than 4 hours, because our backyard was a little less than an acre in size. This was time that was taken away from us, with which we could have done something more worthwhile, like spend time with our child or work on things that generated income—things that mattered. But from the time we enrolled in a lawn-care program through a local service provider, we have not had the need to pull out weeds ourselves. The service provider would proactively treat the lawn with weed and bug control pre-season and educate us on basic lawn care to follow. The time savings have been invaluable, and the weed hog is now an outmoded tool collecting dust in the shed. Investments in just a tool-centric approach to dealing with software security will result in a lot of tools within your companies becoming mere vestigial instruments over time.

To build security in is to proactively follow security processes and implement security controls throughout the SDLC. This means that security requirements are elicited during the requirements phase; and during the design phase, threats are modeled to get an understanding of the attack surface. In development, code is not only written with security controls but also reviewed for security vulnerabilities, verification of the existence of security controls, and the validation of their effectiveness is performed during the testing phase; and when a "go" decision is made at the end of user acceptance testing, process controls are in place to ensure that software is deployed/released with least privilege and other controls that do not nullify the efforts put in during the previous phases. Finally, a post-deployment/release testing and configuration control checks to detect entry points and loopholes, and ensure resiliency post-release, is performed. Figure 1.5 depicts a secure software development life cycle, or Security Development Life Cycle (SDLC) as it is often called.

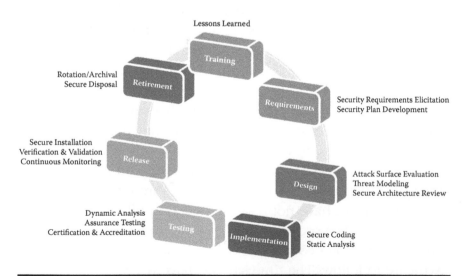

Figure 1.5   Security Development Life Cycle (SDLC).

Building Security In

Proactively following security processes and implementing security controls throughout the software development life cycle.

Irrespective of whether you choose to develop the software using a structured waterfall-like methodology or a piecemeal-based agile methodology, a holistic perspective of incorporating security in the software engineering process must be in place. This includes educating and training your people to implement secure processes that augment security tools.

Build Security In: The Value-Add

When security is built into the software that is developed, the end user or customer not only benefits from getting quality software that is highly reliable (functioning as expected), but one that is also resilient (able to withstand misuse and attacks) and recoverable (able to be restored to normal business operations with minimal disruptions). Figure 1.6 depicts the 3 Rs of software assurance.

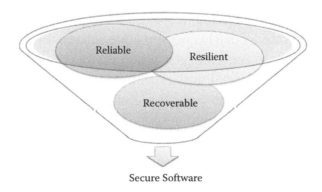

Figure 1.6   The 3 Rs of software assurance.

When the software is reliable, it is less prone to accidental or intentional errors that can occur. The cost of fixing software defects (including security defects) discovered after it has been released is estimated to be significantly greater. In addition to cost savings, when security controls are built into the software, the chances that an attacker can compromise the software or the data it processes, transmits, or stores are minimized. Of course, it would be foolhardy to think that software with security built in is 100 percent resilient to attack, because determined hackers often find a way to break your software. However, making it more difficult for the hacker to exploit your software is necessary, for hackers often try to find the path of least resistance and seek low-hanging fruit.

Conclusion

Software that is built with security proactively built into the SDLC shows the following traits:

- Is reliable, meaning it functions as it is expected to
- Is resilient, meaning it has the ability to withstand misuse and attacks
- Is recoverable, meaning it has the ability to be restored to normal operations upon disruptions
- Is less prone to error
- Is less prone to disclosing sensitive information
- Is available to the end user when needed
- Is built to functional and assurance specifications
- Is less susceptible to logical or semantic flaws
- Meets governance, regulations, compliance (GRC), and privacy requirements
- Has undergone a threat model, and the attack surface is known
- Has a reduced relative attack surface quotient (RASQ) compared to previous versions

- Is defensible against common software attacks
- Has been tested for vulnerabilities
- Is installed with least privilege in hardened hosts
- Is continuously monitored for vulnerabilities and patched as needed
- Securely disposes data and software when it reaches end of life (EOL)

While the bulleted list above lists the qualities of highly secure software when security is proactively built in, the primary reason for software to be built with security in mind is because software assurance is about trust—trust that our customers, clients, suppliers, and other stakeholders have placed on us—and building security in can result in satisfied and happy stakeholders. Quality #1 of highly secure software is that security is built in, not bolted on.

References

"Absolute Sownage — A Concise History of Recent Sony Hacks." *Attrition.org,* 4 June 2011. Web. 19 Oct. 2011. <http://attrition.org/security/rant/sony_aka_sownage.html>.

Anley, Chris, John Heasman, Felix Lindner, and Gerardo Richarte. *The Shellcoder's Handbook: Discovering and Exploiting Security Holes, 2nd ed.* Indianapolis, IN: Wiley, 2007. Print.

"The Ant and the Grasshopper." *Aesop's Fable.* AesopFables.com. Web. 19 Oct. 2011. <http://www.aesopfables.com/>.

Beardsley, David. "Customer Value Driven Development." Cunningham & Cunningham, Inc. Web. 19 Oct. 2011. <http://c2.com/cgi/wiki?CustomerValueDrivenDevelopment>.

Berinato, Scott. "The Cybercrime Service Economy." HBR Blog Network. *Harvard Business Review,* 1 Feb. 2008. Web. 19 Oct. 2011. <http://blogs.hbr.org/cs/2008/02/the_cybercrime_service_economy.html>.

Bertocci, Vittorio. "End to End Security, or Why You Shouldn't Drive Your Motorcycle Naked." *Vibro.NET.* MSDN Blogs,

25 Apr. 2005. Web. 19 Oct. 2011. <http://blogs.msdn.com/b/
vbertocci/archive/2005/04/25/end-to-end-security-or-why-you-
shouldn-t-drive-your-motorcycle-naked.aspx>.

Betjlich, Richard. "No ROI? No Problem." TaoSecurity, 14 July 2007.
Web. 19 Oct. 2011. <http://taosecurity.blogspot.com/2007/07/
no-roi-no-problem.html>.

"Canonicalization, Locale and Unicode." *OWASP Development
Guide.* Open Web Application Security Project (OWASP).
Web. 19 Oct. 2011. <https://www.owasp.org/index.php/
Canonicalization,_locale_and_Unicode>.

Culp, Scott. "10 Immutable Laws of Security Administration."
Microsoft TechNet: Resources for IT Professionals. Microsoft,
Nov. 2000. Web. 19 Oct. 2011. <http://technet.microsoft.com/
en-us/library/cc722488.aspx>.

Kennedy, Susan. "Common Web Application Vulnerabilities."
Computerworld, 25 Feb. 2005. Web. 19 Oct. 2011.
<http://www.computerworld.com/s/article/print/99981/
Common_Web_Application_Vulnerabilities>.

Kumar, Mohit, Ed. "Anonymous Edition." *The Hacker News.* The
Hacker News, Apr. 2011. Web. 19 Oct. 2011. <http://theevil-
hackerz.com/magazine-01-low.pdf>.

"Operation Sony...#OpSony." *Conspiracy Theories, UFOs,
Paranormal, Political Madness, and Other "Alternative Topics."*
AboveTopSecret.com, 3 Apr. 2011. Web. 19 Oct. 2011. <http://
www.abovetopsecret.com/forum/thread684408/pg1>.

Power, Richard and Rik Farrow. "Are You Ready for Electronic
Commerce Crime?" *Network Defense.* Sept. 1997. Web. 19 Oct.
2011. <http://rikfarrow.com/Network/net0997.txt>.

"#RefRef - Denial of Service (DDoS) Tool Developed by
Anonymous." *The Hacker News Network,* 7 July 2007. Web. 19
Oct. 2011. <http://www.thehackernews.com/2011/07/refref-
denial-of-service-ddos-tool.html>.

Rizzo, Juliano and Thai Duong. "BEAST: Surprising Crypto Attack
against HTTPS." *Ekoparty Security Conference,* 23 Sept. 2011.
Web. 19 Oct. 2011. <http://ekoparty.org/eng/2011/juliano-rizzo.
php>.

Romang, Eric. "SUC001: Google Mediapartners Crawlers
Owned? SQL Injection + RFI Detected." Web log
post. *Eric Romang Blog.* ZATAZ.com. Web. 19 Oct.
2011. <http://eromang.zataz.com/2010/04/19/
google-crawlers-owned-sql-injection-rfi-detected/>.

"Secure Sockets Layer (SSL): How It Works." *VeriSign Authentication Services.* VeriSign, Inc. Web. 19 Oct. 2011. <http://www.verisign.com/ssl/ssl-information-center/how-ssl-security-works/>.

Security of Cloud Computing Providers Study. Rep. Computer Associates (CA), Apr. 2011. Web. 19 Oct. 2011. <http://www.ca.com/~/media/Files/IndustryResearch/security-of-cloud-computing-providers-final-april-2011.pdf>.

"SSL Protects Data in Transit, but Not Apps." *Software Quality Information, News and Tips.* SearchSoftwareQuality.com, May 2006. Web. 19 Oct. 2011. <http://searchsoftwarequality.techtarget.com/answer/SSL-protects-data-in-transit-but-not-apps>.

Swanson, Erin. "Top 10 Myths Highlighted on Application Security." Web log post. *Cenzic Security Blog.* Cenzic, 14 July 2009. Web. 19 Oct. 2011. <http://blog.cenzic.com/public/item/236117>.

"USA v. Smak." Cryptome, 31 Aug. 1997. Web. 19 Oct. 2011. <http://cryptome.org/jya/smak.htm>.

Volokh, Eugene. "Security Myths." *SUPERGROUP Magazine,* July 1988. Web. 19 Oct. 2011. <http://www.adager.com/VeSoft/SecurityMyths.html>.

"What Is Paradox of Value?" *Online Business Dictionary.* BusinessDictionary.com. Web. 19 Oct. 2011. <http://www.businessdictionary.com/definition/paradox-of-value.html>.

Wysopal, Chris. "Navigating Cloud Application Security: Myths vs. Realities." *Cloud Security Alliance Blog.* Cloud Security Alliance, 8 Mar. 2011. Web. 19 Oct. 2011. <https://blog.cloudsecurityalliance.org/2011/03/08/navigating-cloud-application-security-myths-vs-realities/>.

Chapter 2

Quality #2: Functionality Maps to a Security Plan

> For which of you, intending to build a tower, sitteth
> not down first, and counteth the cost, whether he
> have sufficient to finish it?
>
> *—Luke 14:28*

Prelude: Breaking the Tape

In my high school days, I was selected to be part of a team of athletes to represent our school in the inter-school athletic events. I participated in the heptathlon events, with the 100-meter and 200-meter sprint events being my favorite. The spectators in the crowd, the expectations of the coach, the atmosphere in the stadium, while exhilarating on the one hand, was at the same time nerve-wracking on the other. And in order to calm the athletes, our coach used to tell us to "focus" and think about breaking the tape at the end of the race. He would want us to think about the race before we even took our starting positions. I must agree that while I first thought that it was quirky to think of a race before it began, every time I played the race in my mind as I assumed the crouching position in the starting blocks, it helped me ease up and focus on the task, which was to complete the race victoriously. Every time I felt the spikes dig into the starting blocks, I used to think of the final step I would take in breaking the tape and winning the race. Not to mention my best timing for the 100-meter dash was a little less than 13 seconds, which earned me the title "The Wonder Boy" in high school. I wonder today as to how I pulled that off. Reminiscing on those glory days, I realize now that our coach had instilled in us young athletes a very valuable principle, which is to begin with the end in mind and to run the race with a plan, not aimlessly.

In a similar manner, when it comes to software security, it is crucially important that the software that is built, is built with a clear understanding of how secure it needs to be when it is finally deployed or released to a customer. Developing software without a clear-cut focus of the security posture in the final product is akin to having a nerve-wracking experience, and the likelihood of success without such a security focus is marginal, if any at all.

Introduction

Quality #2 of highly secure software is that in the software developed, the functionality of the software is mapped to applicable security controls, which in turn are mapped to a plan—a security plan. This implies that a security plan must first exist. Just as any masonry contractor would never pour the concrete for the foundation of a building without first framing it, we must not develop software without first developing the security plan, which provides the framework (or blueprint/template) for how the software will be secured. In fact, from past experience, I would advise that if your company does not have a security plan in place, then you must start your security program by first developing the security plan. One of the primary reasons as to why software today is not hack-resilient is because most software is not developed with a clear understanding of the security objectives (or goals) or a step-by-step implementable security plan. Without this plan, not only would you not be aware of what it takes to secure your software, but also the justification to implement controls by allocating appropriate resources would be extremely challenging.

What Is a Security Plan?

A security plan is one that provides an overview of the security requirements of the software. It describes the controls that exist, or that which must be designed and implemented to address those specified security requirements. In other words, it specifies the *end-state* of how the software must be secured. A security plan is therefore the framework of how to architect secure software.

A security plan can be broken down primarily into four major sections as depicted in Figure 2.1: these include

1. Project information
2. Security requirements

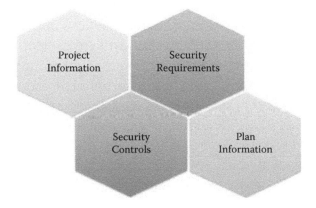

Figure 2.1   Components of a security plan.

3. Security controls
4. Plan Information

Security Plan

The framework of how to architect secure software, which specifies the end-state of how the software must be secured.

The *project information* section covers basic information about the software development project itself. It includes information such as the name of the project (or software being built), the authorized team members, system and information owner, authorizing official for the plan, and categorization of the project based on impact to confidentiality, integrity, and availability. Additionally, it can also include information such as the operational status of the software, its importance to the organization, and a general description of the value (or purpose) that the software will provide to the business or customer.

The *security requirements* section covers the goals and objectives of how the software must be secured. The sources for these requirements can range from internal policy and governance documentation to applicable laws and standards that are externally imposed on the software project, due to the functionality served by the software. For example, if the software that is to be developed is an online e-commerce store that will accept and process credit card information, then your company's confidentiality policy will apply. Additionally, the Payment Card Industry Data Security Standard (PCI DSS) requirements would also apply to the software development project, and this must be identified and documented in the security plan.

The *security controls* section describes the controls that must be present when the software is developed—if they do not already exist. This description must contain the following:

- The title of the control
- How the security control will be implemented
- The responsible person or party for the implementation of the control

These controls may be proactive (safeguards) or reactive (countermeasures) in nature. For ease of tracking within a security plan, these controls are usually grouped into buckets or control classes, for example technical, operational, and management buckets as depicted in Figure 2.2.

Technical controls are those that are enforced by the system or the software itself. These controls support security requirements for data and application by providing automated

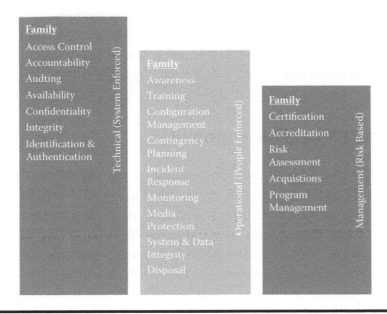

Figure 2.2 Security control classes and families.

protection against misuse and aiding in the detection of security violations. *Operational* controls, on the other hand, are controls that focus on mechanisms that are primarily implemented and executed by people (as opposed to the system or software itself). Operational controls rely on the expertise of the person or party responsible for its implementation, which could be a weak link if the responsible individual or team is not adequately trained in software security. *Management* controls focus on the management of the information system or software so that total risk is managed, and the risk that remains after the implementation of the controls (residual risk) is within the acceptable threshold as expected by the business owner.

The *plan information* section covers the completion and approval dates of the security plan itself. It is important to track this because the security plan must not be a one-time static artifact; rather, it must be dynamically tracked and revisited over the course of the lifetime of the software. These plans are living documents, requiring periodic reviews and modifications to address changing requirements, and procedures must be instituted to keep the plans contextually correct and current.

Security Plan Development

Now that we have an understanding of the components of a security plan, it is important to also know the process by which the plan is developed. Security plan development is a structured activity and requires considerable thought. One must not try to hurry through the process of developing this plan because shortchanging it can result in a plan that is not comprehensive in its coverage of the protection needs of the software.

The security plan development process includes the following steps, as depicted in Figure 2.3.

Figure 2.3   Security plan development.

Step 1: Identify Security Objectives

The first step in the development of a security plan is to identify the security objectives. Security objectives state the expectation and goals of the company as they pertain to assurance of stakeholder trust. A good strategy to start identifying security objectives is to look at the goals as they apply to protection against disclosure (confidentiality objectives), alteration (integrity objectives), and destruction or denial of service (availability objectives). Additionally, it is advised to list these objectives so that they are Specific, Measurable, Achievable, Relevant, and Timely (SMART). For example, it is preferred to list a confidentiality objective as "The software must be architected to prevent the disclosure of sensitive cardholder information during the checkout process" instead of "The software must be architected to maintain secrets."

SMART Security Objectives

These are Specific, Measurable, Achievable, Relevant, and Timely expectations and goals of the company as they pertains to the assurance of stakeholder trust.

Step 2: Identify Applicable Requirements

Once the security objectives are identified, the next step is to identify applicable requirements. These requirements may be externally or internally imposed on the software project. Externally imposed requirements include applicable laws (regulations), compliance, and privacy requirements. Prime examples of this type of requirement in today's landscape are Sarbanes–Oxley (SOX), PCI DSS, and the Gramm–Leach–Blilcy Act (GLBA). Examples of internally imposed requirements include the company's policies and standards. The important task in this step is to identify which of these requirements apply to the software project and which ones do not. For example, if the software does not monitor user activity, then privacy requirements to request user consent using login banners or splash screens would not necessarily apply; or if the software does not collect, transmit, process, or store credit card information, then compliance with the PCI DSS may not be necessary.

Step 3: Identify Threats

Threats to software security can be both from external as well as internal threat agents. Additionally, not all threat agents are necessarily human, as depicted in Figure 2.4. Malicious software (malware) such as proliferative viruses and worms or stealthware such as Trojans, spyware, adware, and rootkits are examples of threat agents that are non-human. Furthermore, not all human threats are caused intentionally, and when identifying threats, accidental threats must also be taken into consideration.

Step 4: Identify Applicable Controls

In the *Art of War,* Chinese military strategist Sun Tzu counsels that if you know your enemy and not yourself, then you can expect to wallow in defeat every time. In the context of software security, if you merely have an understanding of

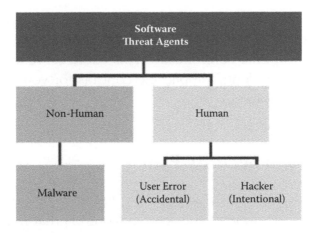

Figure 2.4 Software threat agents categorization. (From Paul, Mano. "Trust in Cyberspace" (ISC)² Whitepaper.)

threats (enemy) without an understanding of controls (your defensive postures), then you can expect to be hacked (wallow in defeat) every time. The next step in the security plan development process is to identify applicable controls. This is a very crucial task to ensure software resiliency.

Know Your Threats; Know Your Controls

If you know your threats (enemy) and not your controls (yourself), expect to wallow in defeat (be hacked) every time.

Once the controls are identified, it is a good idea to classify the controls into their respective control classes (technical, operations, or management). Controls can be further grouped by their security function into families. Some examples of security families include identification and authentication, access control, auditing and accountability, etc. The special publication 800-53 by the National Institute of Standards and Technology (NIST) titled "Recommended Security Controls for

Federal Information Systems and Organizations" highlights a list of security controls broken down by families and classified into the appropriate control class. This could serve as a good starting point to identify applicable controls for your software development project.

Benefits of a Security Plan

Failing to plan is as good as planning to fail. Because the security plan documents the security controls that must be in place, it forms the basis of how software must be secured. It can provide insight into the end-state of security that must be in place before the software is built, making it possible to be proactive about software security. In other words, *the security plan helps you to begin with the end in mind and build security in*, as opposed to bolting on security controls after, or just before deployment. The documented controls can be used to architect and implement authentication and authorization rules when the software is deployed.

The security plan can also provide a valuable guideline for risk management because residual risk is affected by the implementation or lack of implementation of controls. In fact, the very process of selecting the applicable controls to achieve the acceptable levels of risk is a multifaceted risk-based activity.

Furthermore, when a security plan exists and controls are predetermined, then it is relatively easier to conduct certification and accreditation activities. That is, a security plan is a precursor to certification and accreditation (C&A). *Certification* is the comprehensive assessment of technical, operational, and management controls in an information system to determine the extent to which the controls are implemented correctly, operating as intended, and producing the desired outcome with respect to meeting the security requirements documented in the security plan. Certification assessment is performed in support of certification accreditation and gives insight into the secure state of the software or system. When a certification agent validates the *existence* and the *effectiveness* of the security controls implemented in your software, the security plan can serve as the source of requirements for certification. The security plan can be analyzed, updated, and accepted if the controls as per the security plan are present and working as expected in the software. When the controls are implemented and when they operate as expected, residual risk can be determined. Once the residual risk is known, management can officially and explicitly accept the risk to the organization, and this is known as *accreditation*. Management should accredit the software only after a thorough and comprehensive assessment of the controls is completed and if the residual risk is below the acceptable threshold as defined by the business.

C&A can provide insight into any deviations from the expected end-state as documented in the security plan. Knowledge of deviations can prove handy in defending against audit findings in addition to demonstrating due diligence and due care. For example, if the security plan calls for encryption of sensitive information but the certifying agent determines that this cryptographic control is not implementable in the software for some technical reason, then this deviation from the plan can be identified and recorded, along with the reasons for such deviation. When the audit team finds this noncompliance with the plan, it is already a known issue and you can focus on proposing compensating controls, if applicable.

Security plans also help in identifying compensating controls. Compensating controls are those that are used in place of the identified controls when the identified controls are not implementable. Compensating controls, when identified, should provide at least the same degree of protection—if not more—than what would have been provided if the original control were implemented.

Additionally, when security requirements are known and mapped to software functionality, appropriate allocation of resources to implement the controls is relatively easier.

Mapped Software

The task of mapping software to a security plan entails the tying of software functionality to security controls that are documented in a security plan. Because the controls on the plan correlate with threats and with requirements, mapped software has the benefit of knowing which threats are being mitigated and which requirements are being met. Noncompliance with regulatory, privacy and compliance can have detrimental repercussions, and mapped software alleviates this concern.

Given below are two examples to illustrate this quality of mapping controls:

1. *Software functionality:* The software must be able to build a historical evidence of user actions.
   Control(s): Logging, Hashing
   Security requirement: Administrative and business-critical transactions must be logged and the logs must be tamper-proof.
   Objective: Auditing and Accountability.
   Threat(s): Failure to record transactions; alteration of logs.

2. *Software functionality:* Each user must have a unique account with which to interact with the software.
   Control(s): Unique usernames and passwords.
   Security requirement: Remove test and default application accounts (user IDs and passwords) before the software becomes active or is released to the customer. (PCI DSS 6.3.1).
   Objective: Identification and authentication; non-repudiation (accountability).
   Threat(s): Impersonation.

In the first example, the software functionality to be able to build a history of transactions can be tied to the two controls:

logging and hashing. The logging control is mapped to the security requirement of logging administrative and business-critical transactions and the auditing objective. It addresses the threat of failure to record transactions. The hashing control is mapped to the security requirement that the logs must be tamper-proof in accordance with the accountability objective. It addresses the alteration of logs threat. Now with a clear-cut mapping of the software functionality to the controls and requirements documented in the plan, it becomes very easy to address deviations from the plan. For example, if the logging control is implemented as expected but the logs are not protected, then the logs can be altered by a malicious hacker and accountability cannot be assured. Having this map of functionality-to-control-to-requirements brings to light the need to implement both logging and hashing as controls to meet the business objective of the software so that it can provide historical transaction information.

In the second example, the business need for unique user accounts is simply specified as a functional requirement that each user must have a unique account to interact with the software. This functionality can be tied to the unique username and passwords control. This is mapped to the security requirement imposed by the PCI DSS that test and default accounts (user IDs and passwords) must be removed from the software before it becomes active or is released to the customer and the identification and authentication, and non-repudiation (accountability) objectives. This control addresses the threat of impersonation where a user or process can spoof the identity of another and act as if they were the spoofed entity, thereby defeating non-repudiation and accountability assurance altogether. Now, if these test and default accounts are not removed before deployment or release, not only will they provide a potential attack surface for spoofing threats, but this would also violate the functional as well as security requirements specified in the security plan.

From these two simple examples one can see the value that functionality-to-controls-to-requirements mapping provides, and highly secure software has this quality designed into it.

Planning for Security

Failure to plan for security in software is, in essence, planning to fail.

Conclusion

With an increase in the number of security breaches against software today and an increase in the number of attacks or threats, the defenders like you and me often find ourselves falling behind in this race between attackers and defenders. To shift the advantage in our favor, we must start this race with a clear understanding of how to finish it. We must run this race of secure software development with the end in mind so that we can focus, effectively and efficiently, on allocating the limited resources in our organization. Secure software, when developed, clearly demonstrates that the team involved in its development had the end-state of software resilience in mind, and mapped its functionality to the security controls, which in turn is tied to security requirements specified in the security plan. Only with such foresight can we even hope to get the upper hand and, as aforementioned, failing to plan is as good as planning to fail. Software that is deemed secure has a better chance of winning the race between attackers and defenders, unlike others that do not have this quality of being mapped to a plan. Quality #2 of highly secure software is that the software functionality is mapped to a security plan.

References

"Guide for Applying the Risk Management Framework to Federal Information Systems - A Security Life Cycle Approach." NIST Special Publication 800-37 Revision 1, Feb. 2010. Web. 19 Oct. 2011. <http://csrc.nist.gov/publications/nistpubs/800-37-rev1/sp800-37-rev1-final.pdf>.

Los, Rafal. "Why Deer Don't Run & AppSec Programs Fail." *HP Communities.* Following the White Rabbit — A Realistic Blog on Enterprise Security, 14 Jan. 2011. Web. 19 Oct. 2011. <http://h30499.www3.hp.com/t5/Following-the-White-Rabbit-A/Why-Deer-Don-t-Run-amp-AppSec-Programs-Fail/ba-p/2407897>.

Paul, Mano. "Trust in Cyberspace." (ISC)[2] Security Transcends Technology. Web. 19 Oct. 2011. <https://www.isc2.org/uploadedFiles/%28ISC%292_Public_Content/Certification_Programs/CSSLP/TrustInCyberspace.pdf>.

"Payment Card Industry Data Security Standard (PCI DSS) — Requirements and Security Assessment Procedures." PCI Security Standards Council, Oct. 2010. Web. 19 Oct. 2011. <https://www.pcisecuritystandards.org/documents/pci_dss_v2.pdf>.

"Recommended Security Controls for Federal Information Systems and Organizations." NIST Special Publication 800-53 Revision 3, 1 May 2010. Web. 19 Oct. 2011. <http://csrc.nist.gov/publications/nistpubs/800-53-Rev3/sp800-53-rev3-final_updated-errata_05-01-2010.pdf>.

Swanson, Marianne, Joan Hash, and Pauline Bowen. "Guide for Developing Security Plans for Federal Information Systems." NIST Special Publication 800-18 Revision 1, Feb. 2006. Web. 19 Oct. 2011. <http://csrc.nist.gov/publications/nistpubs/800-18-Rev1/sp800-18-Rev1-final.pdf>.

Chapter 3

Quality #3: Includes Foundational Assurance Elements

Therefore whosoever heareth these sayings of mine,
and doeth them, I will liken him unto a wise man,
which built his house upon a rock. And the rain
descended, and the floods came, and the winds
blew, and beat upon that house, and it fell not, for it
was founded upon a rock.

—Matthew 7:24-25

Prelude: What Lies Beneath?

One of the things my wife and I do when we travel is we
bring back home a souvenir that represents the place we
visited. When my beloved wife returned from one of her
trips to Kuala Lumpur, Malaysia, she brought home a model
of the Petronas Twin Towers (known in Malay as the Menara
Berkembar Petronas), which is prominently displayed on our
world travel shelf to remind her of her experience in Malaysia.

As my wife reminisced about the architectural detail and splendor of the Petronas Twin Towers, she described the experience of her visit to the Petronas Twin Towers as a unique, and exhilarating one, that filled her with awe. Rising 452 meters above street level and 88 floors in each tower, the Petronas Twin Towers are the tallest twin buildings in the world and, for a period of time was ranked as the tallest skyscraper in the world. Now, the Burj Khalifa or Khalifa Tower in the United Arab Emirates boasts that title. However, the Petronas Twin Towers are a must-see for any tourist visiting Kuala Lumpur. But what is even more fascinating about this soaring splendor is interestingly hidden from the tourist or its daily tenants. The Petronas Twin Towers not only boast of being the world's tallest twin buildings, but also hold the title of having the world's deepest foundations. Each tower has a foundation that is 4.5 meters thick, containing 13,200 cubic meters of reinforced concrete weighing approximately 32,550 tons, supported by 104 barrette pilings that can withstand huge loads and strong seismic movements (as in the case of an earthquake). The foundation depth is 115 meters. In fact, it is this foundation that lies beneath that even makes it possible for the Petronas Twin Towers to stand erect against potentially destructive natural elements.

In a similar manner, when it comes to software security, when our intent is to develop software that is secure and resilient to potentially destructive threat agents, we must give added attention to the comprehensiveness of the foundations on which the software will be built. We must put first things first, and this entails the inclusion of the foundational elements of software assurance on which the software will be built.

Introduction

Quality #3 of highly secure software is that the software includes in its design, development, and deployment, the foundational assurance elements necessary to make it resilient to hacker attacks. These foundational assurance elements are the must-haves of any software if it needs to withstand the onslaughts of both human and non-human threat agents.

Data: The New Frontier

Before delving into learning about what the foundational elements necessary for software assurance are, let us sidestep for a moment and discuss the importance of data, or information. The primary driver for implementing software security initiatives is the protection of digital assets, and secure software ensures that the digital assets that it uses, processes, or leverages are protected. The main digital asset is data, and software applications are the conduits to it.

President John F. Kennedy used the term "New Frontier" to describe Space in his United States Presidential election acceptance speech when he said,

> We stand today on the edge of a New Frontier – the frontier of the 1960s, the frontier of unknown opportunities and perils, the frontier of unfilled hopes and unfilled threats …

If he were to deliver a redundant speech today, he would find himself delivering a very similar kind of speech, except that "data" would be a major part of this new frontier. If I may take the liberty to write his speech, this is what I would write:

> We stand today on the edge of a New Frontier – the frontier of the early 2000s, the frontier of unknown opportunities [as evident in the business trends] and perils [as evident in bankruptcies being filled], the frontier of unfilled hopes [to tap into newer computing models and data] and unfilled threats [from hacktivism]…

Data is the new frontier in this global economy. The McKinsey & Company report "Big data: The next frontier for innovation, competition, and productivity" rightfully expresses that the amount of data in our world has been exploding so much so that the report refers to this colossal amount of data as "big data." Some of the salient points in this report that highlight the importance of data include the following:

New Frontier

Big Data is the new frontier in global economy, for innovation, competition, and productivity.

---

1. Data has influenced every industry and business function and is now a significant factor of production, alongside labor and capital.
2. Data creates value by one or more of the following ways:
    a. Data makes information more transparent and usable.
    b. Data mining can provide more accurate and detailed information to boost performance and manage inventories.
    c. Data makes it possible to tailor products and services to customers as customer preferences can be uncovered by data segmentation using customer buying trends.
    d. Management can make more meaningful business decisions as trends are uncovered by performing data collection and analysis.
    e. Data can be used for the innovation and creation of next-generation products and services.
3. Data usage will be a key factor for competition and growth of companies. The report states that there is a 40 percent

projected growth in global data generated annually in contrast to only a 5 percent growth in global IT spending.

4. Data provide invaluable benefits to not just companies, but also to consumers. For example, thirty billion pieces of content are shared on Facebook monthly, and this is only expected to increase.

The report further moves on to identify that this explosion in data comes with certain challenges as well. Companies need to establish policies related to privacy, security, intellectual property, and even liability when dealing with data. Access to data will be critical not just from a business perspective, but also from a security perspective.

Data Under Siege

There has been a shift in the types of attacks that are executed against software. In the early days of software attacks, denial-of-service was primarily the outcome, but a majority of the security attacks that are prevalent today have been observed to target data. For example, the SQL slammer worm caused a massive denial-of-service (DoS) by exploiting an overflow in the SQL Server and Desktop Engine database product lines in 2003. But today, we do not see many DoS attacks such as Slammer. Instead, security breaches today predominantly report the loss of data, as was the case with the security breach of T.J. Maxx and Marshalls in 2007, in which more than ten million credit and debit card accounts were possibly stolen, or the 2011 Sony PlayStation Network breach in which more than 100 million user records were stolen.

Data are the target and under siege in many software attacks. The threats to data are primarily of three kinds: disclosure, alteration, or destruction or denial-of-service (DoS).

Foundational Assurance Elements

To secure software, we must put first things first. This means that we must first secure the data by addressing the threats to the data. This is where the foundational assurance elements come in. *Foundational assurance elements* are those security concepts upon which the software must be built to be resilient to hacker attacks. Just as a game of chess has only a finite number of opening sequences—but many other strategies that can be played to win the game—it is imperative to begin the software development project by incorporating the foundational security concepts into its design, development, and deployment.

Foundational Assurance Elements

These are security concepts upon which the software must be built to be resilient to hacker attacks.

The foundational elements are listed below and described in more detail:

- Confidentiality
- Integrity
- Availability
- Authentication
- Authorization
- Auditing

Confidentiality

Confidentiality is the concept of security that ensures secrecy and privacy. Confidentiality controls protect against the threat of disclosure. Any data that is non-public in nature must be protected, for failure to do so can have detrimental to dire consequences. A

World War II American poster best illustrates this with the slogan "Loose Lips Might Sink Ships." This slogan was one of the many that was generated under the campaign "Careless Talk Cost Lives" and it meant that unguarded talk may give useful information to the enemy. The Russians had a similar poster that illustrated "To blab is to help the enemy." Figure 3.1 depicts both the American and Russian posters side by side.

Confidentiality Assurance

Protection against disclosure threats can be achieved using overt and covert secret writing techniques.

Confidentiality assurance can be achieved using *overt* and *covert* secret writing techniques. In overt secret writing techniques such as encryption and hashing, the writing is clearly observed as being disguised, but the information that is being protected is rendered humanly unintelligible or irrecoverable. Covert techniques such as steganography and digital watermarking, on the other hand, attempt to hide the information

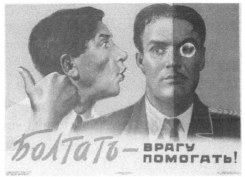

Figure 3.1 World War II American (left) and Russian (right) posters about confidentiality. (From *The News*, Maryland, 1942; V. Koretskii, Careless Talk-Enemy Help, 1951.)

within other media and conceal the very existence of the information itself. Covert techniques are usually used for espionage or intellectual property protection.

In software, the most common form of secret writing is cryptography. Encryption and hashing are cryptographic techniques that are effective in protecting against disclosure attacks when implemented correctly. Encryption is the mechanism by which humanly understandable information (referred to a plaintext or cleartext) that is passed into an algorithm is converted into a humanly unintelligible form (referred to as ciphertext). Along with the algorithm, a unique key is needed to make this conversion. The inverse of encryption is decryption, in which ciphertext is converted to plaintext. When the same key is used for encryption and decryption, it is referred to as *symmetric* key cryptography. When two keys exist for encryption and decryption purposes where the public or the private key can be used for both encryption and decryption, then it is referred to as *asymmetric* key cryptography.

Hashing is the mechanism by which the information that is being protected is passed through a one-way mathematical function and computed into a fixed-length output that looks nothing like the original text. The computed value is known by different terms, such as hash calc value, message digest, or hash sum.

The main distinction between encryption and hashing is that encryption is bi-directional and the original information can be refactored from the disguised information, while hashing is uni-directional and the original information cannot be refactored from the computed hash sum.

Secure software is characterized by having disclosure protection designed and built in. Personal and sensitive information is protected when it is transmitted, processed, or stored by secure software.

When confidential information is transmitted, software that is architected to be highly secure will leverage secure communication protocols such as Transport Layer Security (TLS), Secure Sockets Layers (SSL), or IPSec.

When confidential information is processed, it can be leaked out from memory or cache. Secure software ensures that memory contents are protected from overflow attacks that can lead to compromise and a dump of memory contents. Information in cache can be protected by establishing cache windows with explicit time-to-live settings and encryption.

When confidential information is stored, it must also be protected from unauthorized disclosure. Suppose the software is designed to use stored passwords for authentication purposes; then it is imperative that the stored passwords are protected. Plaintext passwords in data stores are dangerous and provide no defense against the rogue database administrator. Passwords, if stored, must be hashed so that the original value cannot be refactored, instead of being encrypted, in which case someone may be able to decrypt it. However, it must be understood that even hashed passwords can be determined using a table of precomputed hashes. Such a table is referred to as a rainbow table, and rainbow table brute-force cracking can be mitigated by passing a unique nonguessable value, known as the salt, to the hashing function. In such a situation, the attacker may be able to do a rainbow table lookup brute-force attack, but the attacker will not be successful unless he or she also knows the salt value.

In addition to assuring the confidentiality of the information itself, secure software has the quality of protecting all sources of information disclosure. Some of the most common sources of information disclosure include the software make-up configuration files, error messages, and backup or unreferenced files.

The make-up of the software must also be protected. Application settings or sensitive database connection information should be encrypted when it is specified in configuration files as depicted in Figure 3.2.

Error messages must be *laconic*, and exceptions must be handled explicitly. A lot of information can be disclosed

```
<configuration xmlns="http://schemas.microsoft.com/.NetConfiguration/v2.0">
  <configSections>
    <section name="dataConfiguration" type="Microsoft.Practices.EnterpriseLibra
    <section name="securityCryptographyConfiguration" type="Microsoft.Practice:
  </configSections>
  <configProtectedData>
    <providers>
      <add name="MySecretProvider" type="System.Configuration.RsaProtectedConf:
    </providers>
  </configProtectedData>
  <connectionStrings configProtectionProvider="MySecretProvider">
  <EncryptedData Type="http://www.w3.org/2001/04/xmlenc#Element"
   xmlns="http://www.w3.org/2001/04/xmlenc#">
   <EncryptionMethod Algorithm="http://www.w3.org/2001/04/xmlenc#tripledes-cbc'
   <KeyInfo xmlns="http://www.w3.org/2000/09/xmldsig#">
    <EncryptedKey xmlns="http://www.w3.org/2001/04/xmlenc#">
     <EncryptionMethod Algorithm="http://www.w3.org/2001/04/xmlenc#rsa-1_5" />
     <KeyInfo xmlns="http://www.w3.org/2000/09/xmldsig#">
      <KeyName>Rsa Key</KeyName>
     </KeyInfo>
     <CipherData>
      <CipherValue>DzoWHXYC242uON6mnKtyvYQVZEl/NHjQ+zZWdAI52Tc5ztb0gFIlVFzAAaPl
     </CipherData>
    </EncryptedKey>
   </KeyInfo>
   <CipherData>
    <CipherValue>qGM70U1T20m2H/5oogMxxcmhjqAzeMvndiwhUDzon5R3+VBWcDGLB8M8tZ6Xx1
   </CipherData>
  </EncryptedData>
  </connectionStrings>
```

Figure 3.2   Encrypted web.config file.

through verbose error messages, and secure software is characterized by the fact that when the software errors or when an exception occurs, it does not reveal more information than is necessary. Error handling must be designed to redirect the error to a generic handler and limit the information that is displayed to the end user.

Backup and unreferenced files must have proper access control mechanisms in place to limit the exposure of these files to unauthorized individuals as they can contain sensitive information.

Integrity

Integrity is the concept of security that is two-pronged in the protection it provides. The first is that it ensures protection against unauthorized alterations (or modifications or tampering), and the second is that it is a measure of the reliability of the software. Software that is highly secure will perform reliably, meaning that it will perform its operations as expected by the user of the software. For example, if you transfer $1,000 from your checking account to a savings account using the online banking software, you would expect that there is debit of $1,000 from the checking account and a credit of that same amount in the savings account. If you notice that $1,000 has been debited but only $100 was recorded as credit in your savings account, then some unexpected modification has taken place. This could be the case for any of the following reasons:

■ Someone intercepted the transaction and changed it, as would be the case if a man-in-the-middle (MITM) attack had occurred.
■ The software was architected incorrectly, and the variable that holds the amount to be transferred was not set correctly.
■ The design of the database that holds the amount information was not set correctly, and it is leading to truncation of the amount transferred.

Hashing was discussed earlier under the "confidentiality" section, and we learned that it could be used to protect information that should not be refactored, such as passwords, from being disclosed. Although hashing in that context was used as a confidentiality control, it is primarily an integrity control. Hashing can be used to ensure that the data and objects (files, database records) are not tampered with. If the object is modified, then the hash calc value will be different. Secure software will leverage hashing in its design to ensure that it is not tampered with.

Integrity Assurance

Protection against unauthorized alterations and a measure of the reliability of the software.

Figure 3.3 depicts that the SHA256 computed hash values for the text string 'vesper' is ECC9BDDB65DC44516 CA3EAE954EB6D06CBFE4C250CAE103F68D5CF346A7CF703. Now if that text string is changed to 'Vesper' (with the first letter being uppercase), then the SHA256 hash value is different and is 06110F3DD13DF8EDF1CCB65645714D5DC646ED6 EEFBA49DB0773AA67A4AE2392, as indicated in Figure 3.4.

Hash functions also play an important part in the process of making digital signatures. Digital signatures result when the computed hash value of an object is encrypted with the private key of the software publisher. In addition to anti-tampering assurance, should you require authenticity of the software publisher and non-repudiation, then *code signing* can be a viable option, in which the computed hash value of the executable is encrypted with the private key of your organization, resulting in a unique digital signature. The receiving party using your public key can verify this digital signature.

Trust and Validate

While the user can be trusted, user-supplied input should not be, and all user-supplied input must be validated to mitigate a majority of software vulnerabilities.

In addition to hashing, integrity assurance can also be achieved using input validation. Input validation is one of the main controls that addresses a majority of software vulnerabilities such as injection flaws and overflow attacks. Validating that the user-supplied input is legitimate assures information/data integrity. In today's computing environment, input validation is a must-have as input when not validated can be used for malicious activities. In addition to security benefits, input validation is also beneficial to reduce the server

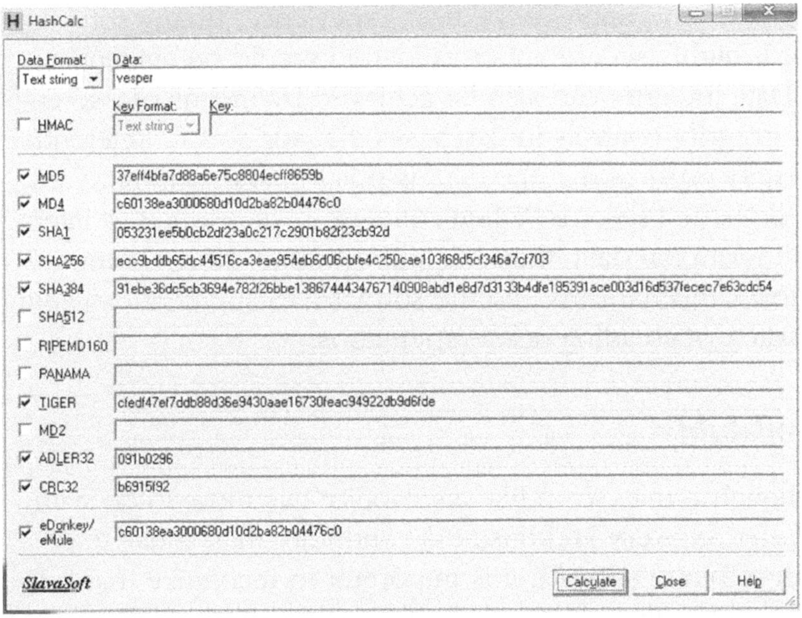

Figure 3.3   Hash calc values for the text string "vesper".

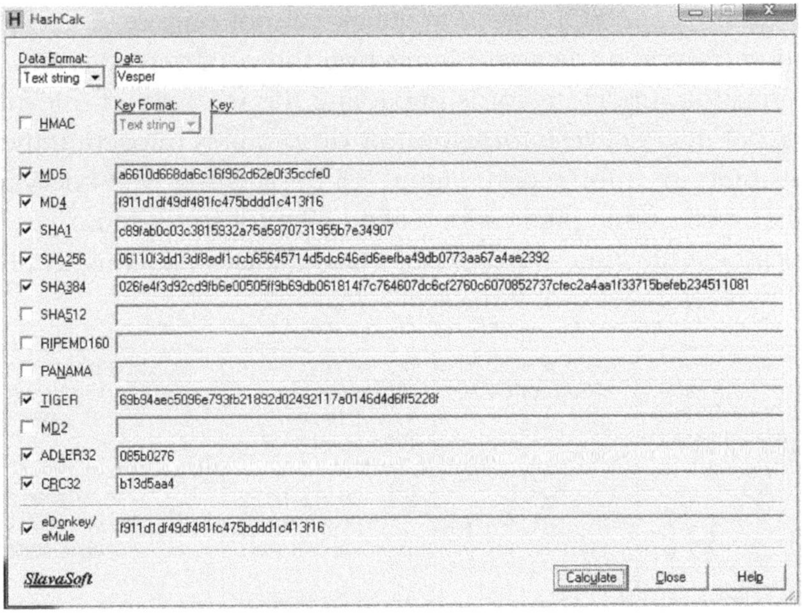

Figure 3.4   Hash calc values for the text string "Vesper".

workload and improve the user experience. In any software that is highly secure, input validation would be evident.

Data integrity can also be achieved by means of referential integrity controls in databases that support it. Referential integrity ensures that the data is pristine and that there are no orphaned records. When software is developed to interact with relational data, then it is important to design commit and rollback mechanisms into the software to augment cascading update or cascading delete operations.

Availability

Although it may seem like availability has more to do with disaster recovery and business continuity than it has to do with software security, it is important to recognize that software with vulnerabilities can cause downtime and business disruptions. The availability of software functionality and the data can be impacted when software is insecurely designed. For example, an SQL injection attack cannot only read information from your database impacting the confidentiality of information, update records impacting the integrity of information, but also delete information or drop tables impacting the availability of information. Figure 3.5 depicts the well-known XKCD web comic publication called "Exploits of a Mom," which best illustrates an SQL injection attack impacting availability with a sense of humor.

Figure 3.5   Example of SQL injection attack impacting availability.
Source: xkcd. http://xkcd.com/327.

Validation and sanitization of input before it is processed by back-end systems can mitigate such availability threats and secure software is characterized by having these controls.

Availability can also be impacted depending on how the software handles failure. In the context of software security, it is preferred to err on the side of caution than otherwise. Secure software is architected to fail secure, meaning that in the event of a failure, digital assets are not put at a risk of compromise.

Err on the Side of Caution

In the event of a software failure, it is important to ensure that digital assets are not put at a risk of compromise.

Fail secure can be accomplished by one of two techniques: fail open or fail closed. In the simplest terms, fail open means that when a failure occurs, the system does not necessarily deny the user their expected operation; whereas, fail closed means that upon the event of a failure, the user is disallowed the continuation of that operation which caused the failure. If the software deals with a physical control system like opening emergency doors, then upon the event of a failure, the software should be designed to fail open, but this is converse to most application security situations. In the majority of software, other than those dealing with life-and-death or physical security solutions, or where the software failure does not negatively impact the security of the system, the software must be architected to fail closed so that the ramifications from the breach upon failure is contained. For example, it would be unwise to architect the software that validates the ATM PIN numbers to allow continued access after three or four incorrect PIN entries. When the software in the ATM machine informs the machine to keep your card on invalid entries above the clipping level, it is an example of fail closed. Many blunders are made if the incorrect decision is made.

Additionally, secure software is designed to handle data replication and load balancing, through commits and roll-backs, so that there is no data integrity or availability issues between the replicated or load balanced systems.

Authentication

Authentication is a security concept that can be best illustrated using the following scenario:

> *User:* I want to get in.
>
> *Software:* Who are you?
>
> *User:* My name is Mano Paul.
>
> *Software:* Can you really prove that?
>
> *User:* Here is my password. It is "s3cr3t".
>
> *Software:* Let me check. That checked out fine but before I let you in, can you provide the additional proof that was sent to your mobile phone?
>
> *User:* Is it 123581321?
>
> *Software:* Let me check. That checked out fine too, but before I let you in, I just need one more thing to be absolutely certain that you are who you claim to be. Can you provide me with your fingerprint?
>
> *User:* Okay, here it is.
>
> *Software:* Thank you. One final check. You are indeed who you claim to be. Come on in.

Authentication is the process of validating and verifying an entity's claim of who they are. The above scenario may seem extensive in software implementation, but it is written here it to demonstrate certain characteristics that you will find in highly secure software. If you pay close attention to the scenario, you will notice that three different factors are being used in verifying the user's claims before entry is granted. The first is the use of a username and password that are both known to the user. This factor is *knowledge* based, which is something that one *knows*. The second is the use of a unique token or identifier that was sent to the user's mobile phone. For the user to be able to supply this requested information, the user must be in possession of that mobile phone. This factor is *ownership* based, meaning that the user must own or possess the device physically before being able to supply the proof. The proof is provided from something that one *has*. The third is the user's fingerprint that is requested. This factor is *characteristics* based, meaning that the claim provided is based on something that one *is*.

Multiple Factors to Consider in Multi-factor Authentication

While multi-factor authentication augments defense-in-depth, if it is designed and implemented without taking into account the end-user's perspective, it can negatively impact psychological acceptability.

Unfortunately, most software today is architected to merely check for just one factor, and the most common one is authentication based on knowledge, such as usernames and passwords. Sadly, this is also the weakest form of authentication when implemented without any *defense-in-depth*. Having more than one factor for authentication purposes is referred to as *multi-factor* authentication. This increases the protection level in the software against spoofing (impersonation) or broken authentication threats. However, it must be recognized that having more than one factor for authentication is often onerous to the end user of the software, and this can negatively impact the *psychological acceptability* design principle. The scenario above shows that it is easy for the user to become frustrated when the software keeps requesting additional claims. Highly secure software is characterized by having this quality of multi-factor authentication for entity claim verification, balanced with psychological acceptability considerations, depending on the criticality of the software or the value of the data that it handles.

Furthermore, authentication breakdowns can cause other serious threats, such as impersonation, session hijacking, session replay, and man-in-the-middle attack to manifest. Such threats are possible when account information, such as usernames and passwords, is exposed in plaintext in the code or configuration files, when passwords and session identifiers are easily guessable, or if the session identifier generation and validation process is not managed. Secure software is characterized by having appropriate session management controls. This means that the session identifiers that are used to track user activities are unique, randomly generated, and nonguessable. Without proper session control, sessions can be hijacked, thereby creating a possible man-in-the-middle attack or replayed, in which case integrity is violated.

Authorization

Authorization is a security concept that goes hand in hand with authentication. It succeeds authentication. It is important to recognize that just because someone is authenticated does not necessarily imply that that person is also authorized to perform the requested operations. For example, when you arrive at an airport, the security agent verifies that you match the photo on your government-issued identifying travel document, be it your passport or your driver's license. If you match, you have been authenticated and you are allowed to enter the airport. But once you are inside the airport, you cannot enter the pilot's lounge to access flight information, even if you tried, unless you are a pilot or have been granted rights as a pilot would be who is operating out of that airport. You need to be authorized (granted the rights and privileges) before you can enter the pilot's lounge. In the same manner, within the context of secure software, the individual or process requesting certain operations in the software must be granted the necessary rights and privileges to perform that requested operation. Authorization is the granting of these appropriate rights and privileges to users and processes.

Without proper authorization controls designed into the software, *least privilege,* which implements the secure design principle of "need-to-know," cannot be enforced. Furthermore, an attacker may be able to exploit the authorization weaknesses in the software and elevate his or her own privilege to that of a super/root user or system administrator. Highly secure software ensures that such privilege elevation is not possible. One way to can ensure this is that secure software will enforce the principle of *complete mediation.* Complete mediation is a secure design principle in which the entity that is requesting access of an object is mediated for authorized permissions, i.e. that is, checked of its authorized privileges and rights, each time and every time, before any operation on the object is allowed.

Authorization Creep

Authorization creep occurs when an individual continues to maintain access rights from previously held roles or positions, and this happens when there are no proper termination access control mechanisms and security management interfaces in the software.

Highly secure software also takes into account *termination access control.* When a user of the software no longer requires access to the functionality of that software, their access to the system, software functionality, and data must be terminated accordingly. Failure to do so can result in what is known as *authorization creep*, wherein individuals continue to maintain access rights from previously held roles or positions within the organization.

Security management interfaces by which you can config-ure the security features within the software must be planned for, designed and implemented, especially if roles based on access control need to be implemented.

Highly secure software will be designed to factor in ter-mination access control and coded to have *security manage-ment interfaces* (SMIs) that can be used to configure access rights and permissions. Figure 3.6 illustrates an example of the Facebook SMI that can be used to manage the permissions of what users can and cannot do.

Auditing

Who or what would make the work of Sherlock Holmes easy? One answer would be Watson; the other is auditing. Like all

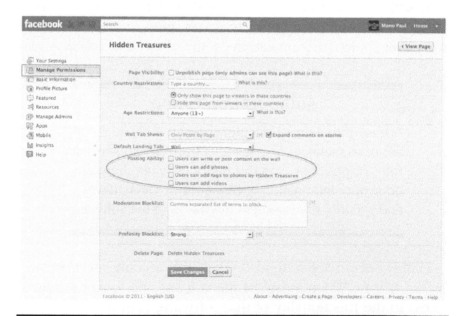

Figure 3.6 **Example of a Security Management Interface (SMI) for managing permissions of a Facebook page.**

the aforementioned concepts, auditing is another foundational element of software security that cannot be ignored when one intends to build and release secure software. Auditing refers to the logging of important business and administrative functionality so that a *history of transactions* can be determined by looking at the logs, if there is a need to. Auditing comes in very handy when one has to provide forensic evidence on the heels of a security breach. Auditing is therefore primarily *detective* in nature. But auditing can also function as a *deterrent* control, because if the users know that their activities are being monitored and logged, they are less likely to do something nefarious.

Sherlock Holmes' Aides

Watson and auditing.

Highly secure software will have auditing capabilities built in. For any important business or administrative functionality, highly secure software will record the fundamental audit fields, which include

1. Who (subject)
2. What (action)
3. Where (object)
4. When (timestamp)

It will be designed to always append to the existing log data and not overwrite it so that historical events can be rebuilt. Additionally, the information that is logged will be in a protected form, usually encrypted to avoid the disclosure of sensitive information from logs. The best approach is not to log sensitive information in log files unless required to do so for the business.

Conclusion

Without a solid foundation, you can expect the structural ability of a building to withstand the onslaughts of nature to diminish over time, until it eventually collapses. In like manner, without the foundational assurance elements of security incorporated into the software, you can expect the resilience

Table 3.1   Foundational Assurance Elements for Software Security

Foundational Assurance Element	Threat Addressed	Control in Software
Confidentiality	Disclosure	Encryption Hashing Steganography Digital watermarking Secure communications Cache protection Protected storage Laconic error messages
Integrity	Alteration	Hashing Input validation Commits and rollbacks Code signing
Availability	Destruction Denial-of-service (DoS)	Input validation Input sanitization Fail secure Data replication Load balancing
Authentication	Spoofing/Impersonation Man-in-the-middle	Multi-factor authentication Unique sessions
Authorization	Elevation of privilege Authorization creep	Need-to-know Termination Access Control Security Management Interfaces
Auditing	Repudiation	Logging Control access to logs

of the software to wane until it gets hacked. We must put first things first, and this means that the foundational elements for software assurance must be considered at the onset of the software development project. The foundational assurance elements, along with the threat that they address and how they can be implemented as a control in software, is summarized and tabulated in Table 3.1.

Quality #3 of highly secure software is that the software includes the foundational assurance elements of security in its design, development, and deployment. Only then can we afford to boast that our software is highly resilient to attacks, because it is built on a rock-solid foundation.

References

Baker, Clyde N., Elliott E. Drumright, Leonard M. Joseph, and Tarique Azam. "The Taller the Deeper." *Civil Engineering (ASCE)* 66.11 (1996): 3A-6A. Print.

McKinsey & Company. "Big Data: The next Frontier for Innovation, Competition, and Productivity." McKinsey & Company, May 2011. Web. 20 Oct. 2011. <http://www.mckinsey.com/mgi /publications/big_data/index.asp>.

Mollin, Richard A. "What Is Cryptography & Why Study It? — A History." *An Introduction to Cryptography*. Boca Raton, FL: Chapman & Hall/CRC Press, 2007. 1–18. Print.

Munroe, Randall. "Exploits of a Mom." Comic strip. Xkcd.com. Web. 19 Oct. 2011. <http://xkcd.com/327/>.

NIST. "An Introduction to Computer Security — The NIST Handbook." *NIST.gov — Computer Security Division — Computer Security Resource Center*. NIST Special Publication 800-12, July 1996. Web. 20 Oct. 2011. <http://csrc. nist.gov/publications/nist-pubs/800-12/800- 12-html/chapter10- printable.html>.

Paul, Mano. "Code (In)Security." (ISC)2 Security Transcends Technology. Web. 19 Oct. 2011. <https://www.isc2.or g/upload-edFiles/%28 ISC%292_Public_Content/Certification_Programs/ CSSL P/CSSLP-WP-5.pdf>.

Stevens, Marc, Arjen Lenstra, and Benne Weger. "Vulnerability of
    Software Integrity and Code Signing Applications to Chosen-
    prefix Collisions for MD5." Technische Universiteit Eiven:
    Wiskunde & Informaticandho, 30 Nov. 2007. Web. 20 Oct. 2011.
    <http://www.win.tue.nl/has hclash/SoftIntCodeSign/>.

Chapter 4

Quality #4: Is Balanced

It is not good to eat much honey.

—Proverbs 25:27

Prelude: The Clown Fish and the Anemone

Growing up, one of my favorite hobbies was aquariums, both freshwater and saltwater. Residents in my home tanks have ranged from the common goldfish and angel fish, to the dangerous piranhas, exotic moray eels, and even an octopus. I have observed several relationships within the aquarium ecosystem—some amicable, while others predatory—but one of the most beautiful relationships observed in a saltwater aquarium is the one between a clown fish and a sea anemone. The clown fish and the sea anemone have a symbiotic relationship.

Symbiosis literally means "living together," and in the symbiotic spectrum there are win-win (mutualism) and win-lose (parasitism) relationships. In mutualism, both the organisms benefit from the other, whereas in parasitism one of the organisms benefits at the expense of the other. The clown fish and the sea anemone have a mutual win-win symbiotic relationship. The clown fish is immune to the poison of the sea anemone and gets its protection from predators by sheltering within the poisonous tentacles of the sea anemone. The sea anemone, on the other hand, gets pickings of food leftover by the clown fish. An example of parasitic symbiosis observed in fishes is that of the tongue-eating louse *(Cymothoa exigua)* that attaches itself to a fish's tongue to suck the blood from it, and atrophies the tongue of the fish over time. There is yet another form of symbiosis and that is commensalism, wherein one organism benefits while the other is neither harmed nor does it benefit. The sessile barnacles that attach themselves to whales or to scallop shells is an example of this, wherein the whale or the scallop is neither benefited nor harmed, but the barnacle benefits from its sessile lifestyle being addressed, getting itself a place to call home and sometimes a ride.

While commensalism may be an acceptable kind of relationship, mutualism is the form of symbiosis that creates a win-win relationship as the perks and benefits are balanced for each of the involved parties. Similarly in the context of software security, there should be a balance that creates a win-win relationship: a balance between risk and reward, between functionality and assurance, and between threats and controls.

Introduction

Quality #4 of highly secure software is that the software is balanced—in terms of its risk and reward, functionality and assurance, and threats and controls.

Balancing Scale: Risk and Reward

Although the security team may be "gung-ho" about securing a company's digital assets, which include the software developed within the company, the language that is spoken in the boardroom is a little different; and unless the security team members can learn to talk that talk, it is highly unlikely that they will be successful in helping the company develop secure software.

Discussion in the boardroom centers around three major themes:

1. How are we going to increase our value?
2. What do we need to pay to earn value?
3. What are the issues that can prevent us from increasing our value?

Discussions in a security team meeting also center around three major themes:

1. What are the things we need to protect?
2. What resources would be necessary to protect our assets?
3. What are the issues that can prevent us from protecting the assets as required?

While on the surface it may seem like the boardroom and the security team have different objectives, interestingly, closer scrutiny of these themes reveals that both the boardroom and the security team in fact have very similar goals. Let me explain. "How are we going to increase our value?" (board-room question) and "What are the things we need to protect?" (security team question) are both about *assets*. The value of a company comes from the assets it has or generates. These assets may be tangible assets such as servers, software, monies, etc., or intangible such as company brand, goodwill, reputation, etc. This is, in essence, really about *return,* the return on investment (ROI). Without the appropriate protection of these assets, the company may in fact lose even the value that it has. Second, "What do we need to pay to earn value?" (board meeting question) and "What resources would be necessary to protect our assets?" (security team question) both have to do with *cost*. Earning value and protecting assets may not be overly expensive with proper planning, but it is certainly not free. A conscious decision to allocate appropriate human and financial resources for the protection of assets is important and necessary. This is, in essence, really about *investment*. Finally, "What are the issues that can prevent us from increasing our value?" (boardroom question) and "What are the issues that can prevent us from protecting the assets as required?" (security team question) both have to do with things that threaten the realization of the expected value. This is, in essence, really about *risk*. Table 4.1 illustrates the similarities between what the boardroom objectives and the security team's objectives are in terms of assets, costs, and risk.

The language that the business speaks is primarily in terms of return, investment, and risk, and security teams need to speak likewise. Companies that have recognized this not only have a good understanding of the assets that need protection, but also plan in advance to allocate appropriate time and resources to address any threats that may threaten the value of the company. Such companies generate highly

Table 4.1 Similarities Between Objectives from the Board Room and the Security Team

Objectives		Concept
Board Room	*Security Team*	
How are we going to increase our value?	What are the things we need to protect?	Assets
What do we need to pay to earn value?	What resources would be necessary to protect our assets?	Cost
What are the issues that can prevent us from increasing our value?	What are the issues that can prevent us from protecting the assets as required?	Risk

secure software because the software that is developed has the appropriate allocation of time and resources *(investment)* to build in controls and gain the benefits *(return)* of increased resiliency and reduced attack surface *(risk)*. An observable characteristic of software that is developed by balancing reward with risk is that the software is not only certifiable but it can be accredited as well, because the risk is known and understood.

Security Lingo

The language that the business speaks is primarily in terms of return, investment, and risk; and security teams need to speak in such a manner as well, to be effective.

Balancing Scale: Functionality and Assurance

The article titled "Balancing Act: Security Vs. Functionality," which was published at GovInfoSecurity.com, features an interview between Richard "Dickie" George, the technical director of the National Security Agency (NSA) Information Assurance Directorate, and Eric Chabrow, the Executive Editor of GovInfoSecurity.com. It highlights this need that as more functionality is added to information systems and applications, the opportunity for hackers also increases. George stated in his interview that, "It is a real trade off. You always want the functionality and you always know you are providing opportunities so you need to take that into account and try to build in additional security every time. It is a race." And when asked, "Are we winning the race so far?" his response was, "We are not losing."

Unfortunately such an affirmative response is not the case in many companies, and yours may be one of them. Dissecting these companies' mindset to software development would reveal that they may be software powerhouses, but they give little or no thought to the assurance aspect of the software they build. The reason for such an imbalance between functionality and assurance is primarily driven by the constraints imposed by what is referred to in project management as the *iron triangle*. The iron triangle consists of three constraints and is therefore also referred to as the *Triple Constraints*. The three constraints in managing any project, including a software development project, are scope, schedule, and cost, as depicted in Figure 4.1.

Balancing Act: Security Vs. Functionality

"It is a real trade off. You always want the functionality and you always know you are providing opportunities so you need to take that into account and try to build in additional security every time. It is a race."

Richard 'Dickie' George
Technical Director, NSA

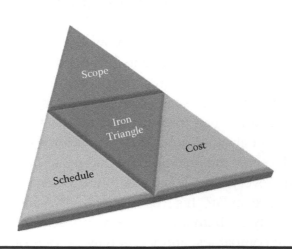

Figure 4.1   The iron triangle.

Scope includes all the work that must be completed in order to deliver the software product or service at the expected levels of quality. In other words, it is all the *functionality* that must be completed within the software to provide a solution to the business problem in hand, at the level of quality that is expected by the business. *Schedule* is the duration that is needed to complete the required functionality defined in the scope of the project. It is the *time* in hours, days, months, or years that is captured in a project plan. *Cost* is the sum of all the direct and indirect charges incurred during the course of the project. It includes the labor costs, which is the amount of money that it would take to pay the staff in the project and any other related costs such as travel, hardware, software, legal fees, escrow fees, etc.

One cannot change one component of the iron triangle without affecting the other. For example, increased scope will lead to more time and more cost; or if cost remains the same and the project deadline is moved earlier, then scope will be impacted. Being governed by such stringent constraints, security, which is often a nonfunctional attribute for the business, gets left on the sidelines, leaving the software vulnerable to exploitation. This is what we must try to avoid, and software that is highly secure does not ignore the assurance capabilities when implementing functionality.

It must also be understood that in today's computing world, there are other constraints that can be imposed on a project in addition to scope, schedule, and cost. This is leading to what is referred to as the death of the iron triangle. With a move toward agile computing methodologies such as extreme programming or Scrum, the schedule and cost are often fixed, while the scope is not quite as defined within each sprint. The extent of functionality implemented is often a measure of the team's productivity. In other words, say that you will place four junior-level software developers at a fixed rate per hour (cost) to develop your billing and shipment tracking software within the next four weeks (time); then the scope of requirements that gets done depends on the experience and knowledge of the team members. The productivity of this project will vary if the same project is staffed with four senior-level software developers. In agile programming, although the overall project scope is captured in the product backlog, the scope within each timebox or sprint cycle is not as rigid as it used to be under traditional deliverable-based software development methods.

To have a win-win situation when developing software, the functionality of the software should be balanced with the assurance capabilities of the software. We cannot afford to ignore the security aspects of the software and lose this race. It is advised that the assurance capabilities of the software (i.e., the controls that are proactively built in) are also tracked as core functionality in the software development project so that they are not ignored nor deferred for future releases. Highly secure software will balance the assurance aspects of the software with its functionality.

Balancing Scale: Threats and Controls

When I was in middle school, I was bullied by some youth from the neighboring village and was beaten badly. The very next month I joined the Karate school to learn self-defense; and since then, I have always been involved in some form of martial arts. After spending over half a decade of learning karate, I joined a Taekwondo school and studied that art form for a couple of years. Currently, I am enrolled in the Shaolin Do Kung Fu School in Austin, Texas, along with my five-year-old son, Reuben. In a couple of years, we expect to have our black belts.

In all these martial arts, one of the first things I was taught was how to stand in the right posture. Our instructor, Senior Master Joe Schaefer, 7th degree black belt, who is the founder and owner of the Austin Shaolin Do Kung Fu school and a student of Grandmaster Sin Kwang The, also has a Doctorate in Neuroscience. As his students, we get to learn from him not only the physical motions of the Shaolin Do art form, but also the mental aspects that go with it. He states,

In martial arts, the stance you choose to fight from is a strategic choice of where you allocate resources. This determines whether you can react quickly to attacks from any direction, are mobile or stationary with a stable counter defense. Success or failure starts with the stance you choose!

Senior Master Joe Schaefer
7th degree Black Belt

In the article titled "The Peaceful Dragon—The Four Right Reasons for Stance Training" Master Eric Sbarge highlights that one of the primary purposes of stance training is to develop a solid root, while the other three reasons are to improve posture, to have a tempered (calm and controlled) mind, and to cultivate the inner energy or *chi*. To develop a *solid root*, means you can take any posture and remain stable in it, just as a rooted tree does not budge under the onslaughts and forces of natural elements. The idea behind stance training is so that you can become rooted in each and every posture, whether you are defending or attacking. In addition to stability, rooting allows agility from sweeping attacks. It helps you allocate your energy and power for immediate and effective counterattacks. *Stance training is about balance; balancing the attacks with appropriate stability and counterattacks.*

In likewise manner, when it comes to software security, it is crucial to develop our software to be stable so that it does not topple over when under attack and agile to respond with effective countermeasures when attacked. Such *stability* and *agility* will give the software the ability to enforce controls immediately and effectively mitigate any damage. The success or failure of an attacker's exploit against your software starts with the stance (posture) your software takes in its design, development, and deployment.

Secure software is characterized by balancing threats with controls so that it is rooted against hacker exploits. This means that for every perceivable threat, identified using a threat model, there exists one or more controls to address that threat. For example, to address the threat of Cross-Site Scripting (XSS), controls such as output encoding, request validation, use of InnerText properties of controls, disallowing active scripting, etc., are in place. Table 4.2 depicts controls that can be used to protect against the most common application threats, when designed and implemented in the software.

As you may have noticed, for each threat one or more controls can be designed or implemented. It may also be observed that some controls can address more than one type of threat. For example, the implementation of account locking clipping levels can be used to address authentication attacks and/or brute-force threats. It is important to ensure that threats to software are neutralized using the appropriate controls. Highly secure software is characterized by balancing threats with the appropriate design and implementation of controls.

Conclusion

Quality #4 of highly secure software is that the software is balanced, i.e., it is developed with consideration of risk and reward; with the functionality of the software balanced with its assurance capabilities and with controls designed and implemented to neutralize threats.

Table 4.2 Balancing Threats with Controls

Threat	*Controls*
Overflow (buffer, integer)	Validate input (length/size) Check memory buffer boundary size Disallow deprecated/banned API Compile code with memory protection switches if feasible (e.g., gs flag) Use Address Space Layout Randomization (ASLR) Use Data Execution Prevention (DEP)
Injection flaws	Use safe API, which avoids the use of the back-end interpreters Use parameterized queries Use prepared statements Disallow dynamic query construction Validate input using white lists Escape/encode user-supplied input Use generic error messages Remove unused/extended procedures or functions
Cross-site scripting (XSS)	Encode output Escape untrusted user-supplied input Validate requests and input using white lists Use InnerText properties of controls Disallow active scripting Use browser context security policy if supported
Authentication attacks (bypass, spoofing, etc.)	Implement multi-factor authentication Cryptographically protect credentials Encrypt cookies Implement account lockout clipping levels
Session attacks (session hijacking, session replay, man-in-the-middle, etc.)	Use hardware-based tokens User-specific sessions Use transport layer protection (e.g., SSL/TLS) Use network layer protection (e.g., IPSec)

(Continued)

Table 4.2 (Continued)   Balancing Threats with Controls

Threat	Controls
Insecure direct object reference	Validate parameters Encapsulate internal objects Index internal objects and implement referencing Hash or encrypt Query String values Implement complete mediation
Cross-site request forgery (CSRF)	Implement unique tokens per request or session Use non-guessable (random) session identifiers Implement explicit logout functionality Verify Referrer Origin of Request Use POST instead of GET method
Security misconfiguration	Remove default accounts and passwords Disable ports, protocols, and services Patch software Harden hosts Implement periodic scanning
Insecure cryptographic storage	Cryptographically secure data at rest Do not hardcode cleartext passwords in code Cryptographically protect backups and archives Use proven and vetted standard algorithms Use cryptographically strong keys
Brute-force attacks (password cracking, failure to restrict URL, etc.)	Implement multi-factor authentication Implement account lockout clipping levels Use unique salt in hashing function Implement Role-Based Access Controls (RBAC) Validate URL requests White list URLs Obfuscate URL schemes
Insufficient transport layer protection	Implement transport layer protection (e.g., SSL/TLS) Set "secure" flag on all sensitive cookies Use FIPS 140-compliant algorithms Implement proper certificate management

Table 4.2 (Continued)   Balancing Threats with Controls

Threat	*Controls*
Unvalidated redirects and forwards	Avoid using parameter-based redirects and forwards Validate that the user is authorized to access the destination address Map destination parameters to an index or reference value instead of the actual URL
Information disclosure attacks (verbose error messages, unhandled exceptions, social engineering, etc.)	Use nonverbose error messages Handle exceptions explicitly Redirect errors to a generic error page Encrypt the cache Implement user awareness Disable HTML-formatted e-mails SPAM control
Malicious file execution attacks	Implement sandboxing Implement quarantining Implement hardening Implement indirect object referencing Validate file content (not just filename extensions) Implement binary analysis of uploaded content
Denial-of-service attacks	Implement load balancing Implement replication
Repudiation attacks	Implement logging and auditing Implement code signing

Just as the best chefs know how to infuse additional flavors into the right proportion of ingredients at the right time without losing the flavor, when security features are infused into the software that is built, it must not lose any business functionality. We must think win-win, and this means that software that is developed is not prone to being exploited, while providing the service that is expected by the business. It must be rooted and stable so that it does not get swept over by threats that manifest.

Without the appropriate levels of security controls built into the software, the balancing scales would tip on the side of the hackers, but highly secure software aims to tip the scales back in your favor.

References

Chabrow, Eric. "Balancing Act: Security Vs. Functionality." GovInfoSecurity.com, 14 Dec. 2009. Web. 20 Oct. 2011. <http://www.govinfosecurity.com/articles.php?art_id=2005>.

Day, Heather M. "Fiscal Sponsorship: Symbiosis in Action." *Conservation Connect,* 13 July 2011. Web. 20 Oct. 2011. <http://conservation-connect.org/2011/07/13/fiscal-sponsorship-symbiosis-in-action/>.

"OWASP Top Ten." *Open Web Application Security Project (OWASP),* 19 Apr. 2010. Web. 20 Oct. 2011. <https://www.owasp.org/index.php/Category:OWASP_Top_Ten_Project>.

Sbarge, Eric. "The Peaceful Dragon — The Four Right Reasons for Stance Training." *The Peaceful Dragon.* Web. 20 Oct. 2011. <http://www.thepeacefuldragon.com/stancetraining.shtml>.

Snyder, Ben. "The Death of the Project Management Triangle." *PM Hut,* 29 Oct. 2009. Web. 20 Oct. 2011. <http://www.pmhut.com/the-death-of-the-project-management-triangle>.

"Tongue Eating Parasite That Becomes The Fish's Tongue." *TwistedSifter.com,* 13 Sept. 2009. Web. 20 Oct. 2011. <http://twistedsifter.com/2009/09/tongue-eating-parasite/>.

Chapter 5

Quality #5: Incorporates Security Requirements

> A wise man will hear, and will increase hearing;
> and a man of understanding shall attain unto wise
> counsels.
>
> —*Proverbs 1:5*

Prelude: Lost in Translation

When trying to teach our son, Reuben, about the importance
of listening, my beloved wife Sangeetha and I use a rhyme
about a wise old owl. The lyrics of the rhyme are as follows:

> A wise old owl lived in an oak.
> The more he saw the less he spoke.
> The less he spoke the more he heard.
> Why can't we all be like that wise old bird?

During World War II, the United States Army used this
rhyme to illustrate that "Silence means Security" on a poster
and changed the last line to read "Solider ... be like that
old bird!"

In the context of software security, often silence truly means security. This is so, not just from a confidentiality angle, but also from the fact that when one seeks to understand the security requirements by speaking less and listening more, then the software is more likely to demonstrate the reliability (functioning as expected and designed), resiliency (ability to withstand attacks), and recoverability (ability to restore back to normal operations when breached) aspects of software assurance.

Furthermore, when the security requirements are not properly understood before the software is designed and implemented, there is a greater tendency that the assurance aspects of the software will be lost in translation. The apocryphal gag from World War I about a group of British soldiers who sent a message back to their headquarters, which when it reached the intended authorities, through the command chain had been lost in translation, best illustrates this. The soldiers had sent the message "Send reinforcements, we're going to advance." This message was passed from one person to another down the trenches before it reached headquarters. The message that was conveyed at the headquarters was "Send three and fourpence, we're going to a dance."

Unfortunately, more often than we would like, such communication failures do actually occur in our industry, especially within the context of software development projects, and are one of the main reasons for the vulnerabilities that exist in our software. When security requirements are not comprehensively identified, understood, and traceable, then the likelihood of the software being resilient to hacker attacks dwindles.

Introduction

Quality #5 of highly secure software is that the software incorporates security (assurance) requirements, in addition to the business (functional) requirements, appropriately and adequately. In other words, highly secure software takes into account the various *types* of requirements and the development life cycle incorporates different *techniques* to elicit and implement security requirements. Furthermore, in highly secure software, the security functionality is *traceable* to the business and other functional requirements. In simple terms, highly secure software is developed after the development team members have sought to understand the varied requirements, before they expect the business end user to understand the security features that are implemented. They seek first to understand, and only then to be understood.

Software Security Requirements

Without software requirements, software will fail. Without software security requirements, software will get hacked.

Without software requirements, software will fail; without software security requirements, software will get hacked. Earlier we learned that highly secure software maps to a security plan. The security plan provides an overview of the security requirements of the software. But, where do these software security requirements come from? What are the different types of security requirements? How do we identify and glean security requirements for the software? How and why do we document these security requirements? The following section answers these questions in more detail.

Types of Software Security Requirements

One of the first steps that a company, intending to develop highly secure software, must do is to be aware of the various types of applicable security requirements. Taking a structured look at each of the sources of security requirements and determining their applicability to the software being developed is crucial for designing, developing and deploying hacker-resilient software.

Some security requirements are *externally* imposed while others are *internally* mandated as depicted in Figure 5.1. Highly secure software factors into its design, development, and deployment all these sources of security requirements.

Externally imposed security requirements are usually from

- *Regulations and compliance.* These requirements include those with which your company must comply. Depending on the legal environment in which your company operates, certain regulatory requirements may be imposed that the company cannot ignore, because ignoring these requirements can have serious repercussions on the company. Some examples include:
  - Sarbanes-Oxley Act (SOX), which applies to publicly trading organizations in the Securities Exchange Commission. Section 404 of the Act, which is most closely related to information security, requires

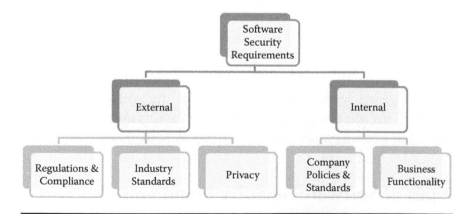

Figure 5.1   Sources of software security requirements.

management to assess and report on the effectiveness of internal control over financial reporting.
- Health Insurance Portability and Accountability Act (HIPAA), which applies to health-care providers, mandates that personal health information (PHI) is protected.
- Gramm-Leach-Bliley Act (GLBA) and Basel II, which apply to banking and financial institutions, mandate the protection of nonpublic information against disclosure or alteration by unauthorized parties. GLBA also prohibits conflict-of-interest responsibilities of personnel, therefore ensuring separation of duties. For example, an officer, director, or employee of a securities firm cannot also simultaneously serve as an officer, director, or employee of a member bank.
- Federal Information Security Management Act (FISMA), which applies to the United States federal agencies, mandates the protection of economic and national security interests of the United States of America.
- European Union (EU) Data Protection Directive mandates the protection of personal data in the EU.
- Canadian Personal Information Protection and Electronic Documents Act (PIPEDA) is the equivalent of the EU Data Protection Directive, which mandates the protection of personal data in Canada.
- California civil code 1798.82 (commonly referred to as State Bill 1386), and Massachusetts 201 CMR 17.00 are examples of state laws that mandate that the companies must inform the residents of the state whose information is breached or leaked.

The company must take into account the local laws of regions and countries where the software is developed or services rendered.

■ *Industry standards.* Industry standards are those requirements that apply to a particular industry and must be
factored into the software being developed. Some of
these standards are developed by international standards bodies such as the International Organization for
Standardization (ISO) or domestic standards bodies such
as the National Institute of Standards and Technologies
(NIST). Although internal company standards are manda-
tory by definition, industry standards are not necessarily
so. Some examples include
  – ISO 27000 series or the Information Security Management
    Systems family of standards provides best practice recom-
    mendations on managing information security systems,
    risks, and controls within the organization.
  – In some cases, depending on the data being processed,
    certain standards may be applicable. For example, soft-
    ware that collects, transmits, processes, and stores card
    holder data will need to comply with the Payment Card
    Industry Data Security Standard (PCI DSS). The PCI DSS
    in its current version explicitly calls for the need to build
    and maintain secure applications in its requirements.
  – The Special Publications 800 series (SP 800) published
    by NIST provides documents of interest to the com-
    puter security community. SP 800-64 is of particular
    importance to the software security community as it
    is about the security considerations that must be taken
    into account in the System Development Life Cycle
    (SDLC). Software that is deemed secure would factor in
    the recommendations provided in this publication.
  – Organization for the Advancement of Structured
    Information Standards (OASIS) drives the development,
    convergence, and adoption of open standards for the
    global information security. They promote industry con-
    sensus and produce worldwide standards for security,
    cloud computing, Service Oriented Architectures (SOA),
    Web services, the Smart Grid, electronic publishing,

emergency management, etc. Some of the standards that OASIS publishes that are of particular interest and application to software development include the Application Vulnerability Description Language (AVDL); eXtensible Access Control Markup Language (XACML); Key Management Interoperability Protocol Specification; Security Assertion Markup Language (SAML); Universal Description, Discovery and Integration (UDDI); and Web Services Security.

■ *Privacy.* Privacy requirements are those that mandate the protection of an individual's personal information against disclosure. The data protection directives and laws can be extrapolated to provide privacy requirements but the Children's Online Privacy Protection Act (COPPA) is an example of an act that explicitly calls out privacy requirements. COPPA makes it unlawful for an operator of a website or online service directed to children (under the age of thirteen) to make their personally identifiable information (PII) publicly available, through the Internet or through a homepage of a website, a pen pal service, an electronic mail service, a message board, or a chat room. Your company may have privacy policies that need to be factored into the software as well.

Additionally, when *anonymity* must be assured, the software that is collecting the information must be architected to provide "unlinkability," meaning that the provider of the information cannot be identified with (linked to) the information provided. When you need to protect against network surveillance and traffic analysis on the Internet, Tor (The Onion Routing), which assures privacy over public networks, can be used. Tor enables software developers to create new communication tools with built-in privacy features. It provides a platform on which software developers can build new applications with built-in anonymity and privacy, and allows companies and individuals to share information over public networks without compromising their privacy.

Assuring Privacy

Anonymity and Unlinkability must both be ensured
to assure true privacy.

Internally mandated security requirements are usually from

■ *Company policies and standards.* Just like many companies that have a plethora of internal policies and
standards that impact software development, it is
quite possible that your company also has a few. This
governance documentation can be used to determine
the security requirements that must be factored into the
software to assure its resilience. Examples of such policies
and standards include the data classification policies,
acceptable use policies, export control policies, open
source usage policy, enterprise patch management policy,
and the application coding standard.

If your company does not have these policies or standards in effect, you are well advised to first develop and
implement these policies and standards before attempting
to interject processes and technologies to build security
into the software.

■ *Business functionality.* One of the most important and
primary sources of security requirements is the business
functionality itself that the software must provide. In fact,
depending on the business functionality, various other
requirements from other sources may become applicable.
For example, if the software being developed will have
e-commerce functionality, collecting and processing cardholder information, then the PCI DSS becomes applicable
and disclosure protection controls such as encryption or
hashing may need to be designed and implemented. If
the business functionality calls for auction-like capabilities

in the software, then timing and sequencing requirements must be identified and implemented so that race conditions do not occur.

Highly secure software teams first seek to understand the business requirements before seeking to be understood. The well-known Chinese proverb that states "Tell me and I'll forget; show me and I may remember; involve me and I'll understand" is applicable in the context of engaging the business to determine security requirements.

BASS BAIT

Business Aware Information Technology (BAIT) teams seek to understand the business requirements first by engaging the business user in the development of Business Aware Secure Software (BASS).

Now it is important to recognize that not all security requirements need to be explicitly evident to the business user. For example, the design of the software should factor in the design principle of *psychological acceptability,* making the security implementation easy to use and transparent to the business end user, because subjecting the end user to full details of how the security controls are implemented can run the risk of the end user circumventing the protection that the controls provide, especially if it is too burdensome for the end user to follow.

Techniques to Elicit Software Security Requirements

In addition to the factoring in the varied types of security requirements, highly secure software is also characterized by having gone through structured requirements elicitation processes. All security requirements may not be *explicitly* stated in these above-mentioned sources. Some of them are *implicit* and may need to be inferred using certain elicitation techniques. The requirements elicitation process aims to translate governance, regulatory, compliance, privacy, policies, standards, and functional requirements into security requirements. The most common secure software requirements elicitation processes include policy decomposition, data classification, subject/object modeling, and abuse case modeling.

Policy decomposition is the process of breaking down high-level policy requirements into security objectives and eventually protection needs and secure software requirements. It gives us insight into the governance requirements as they pertain to regulations, compliance, privacy, etc. *Data classification* is the process of grouping the data into appropriate categories based on the impact of threats that disclose (confidentiality), alter (integrity), and destroy (availability) data. It is then used to identify and prioritize the appropriate levels of secure software controls that will be built in. As you may be aware, it would be necessary for the software to protect data classified as top secret over public directory information, but the extent of protection is dependent on the classification of the data itself. Data that are classified as "top secret" require even greater protection against disclosure than data that are just classified as "secret" or "sensitive." The *subject/object modeling* process allows us to identify relationships and constraints between the requestor (subject) of the service and the requested resource (object) that can render the requested service. Having the subject-to-object relationships mapped out helps identify the access control rules that must be enforced in the software. *Abuse case modeling* is the process of determining the unintended behavior of the software. It is sometimes referred to as misuse cases and views the software from a threat agent (hackers) perspective. It helps identify the negative and detrimental scenarios by which the threat agent will exploit the software and the consequences when the threat agent is successful. Having an understanding of how someone can abuse the software can help us identify the security controls that must be built in to mitigate the threats. Figure 5.2 illustrates the common security requirements elicitation processes and how they can help us develop highly secure software. Software that is deemed highly secure would have undergone these processes in the requirements analysis phase of the software development life cycle.

Formal requirements engineering techniques such as the Security Quality Requirements Engineering (SQUARE) methodology and the Comprehensive, Lightweight Application Security Process (CLASP) can help software development teams build security into the early stages of existing and new software development life cycles in a structured, repeatable, and measurable way.

SQUARE is a nine-step process that begins with identifying and assessing processes and techniques to improve requirements identification, analysis, specification, and management, and focuses on management issues associated with the development of good security requirements. Figure 5.3 depicts the nine-step process of the SQUARE methodology.

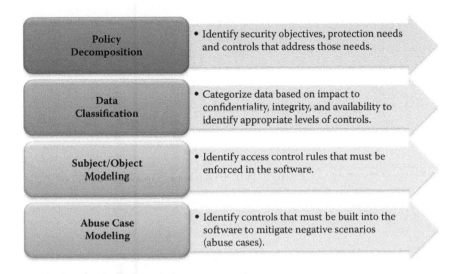

Figure 5.2   Security requirements elicitation techniques.

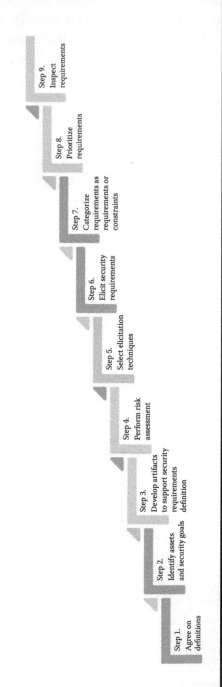

Figure 5.3 SQUARE methodology.

CLASP is the result of extensive field work in which the system resources of many development life cycles were broken down to generate a comprehensive set of security requirements.

To develop highly secure software, it is well advised to choose and follow a structured requirements engineering process that incorporates security requirements early on in the SDLC. Whether you choose to use formal methodologies such as SQUARE or CLASP is left to you.

Traceability of Software Security Requirements

Highly secure software is also characterized by the quality of allowing one to trace the security requirements back to functional or governance requirements. This implies that not only is the software functionality documented in a requirements traceability matrix, but also that the security requirements are documented.

Documentation of security requirements in a traceability matrix provides the following benefits:

- The ability to identify deviations
- The ability to justify the allocation of resources for the development of security features
- Provides a starting point to generate test cases, both functional and security related

Requirements to Retirement

It is important to recognize that while it is necessary to elicit security requirements in the requirements phase of the SDLC, it is equally important to ensure that these security requirements are designed, implemented, and configured correctly throughout the SDLC. This means that from requirements until retirement, security requirements are incorporated into the software. For example, if it is determined to design the software with need to know and least privilege, but just before release, you learn that due to disparate configurations between the development and the production or user environment, the software must be configured to run with elevated privileges, then configuring the software to run as an administrator will nullify all the protection efforts that were taken earlier. It is therefore imperative to incorporate security requirements from the requirements phase to the release phase, and eventually the retirement (disposal) of the software itself.

Requirements to Retirement

From requirements until retirement, software security requirements must be incorporated into the software.

Conclusion

Quality #5 of highly secure software is that the software incorporates security requirements comprehensively throughout the life cycle. The phrase "dot your i's and cross your t's" is used to mean that those who dot their i's and cross their t's deal with all the details, no matter how trivial some may seem, when doing something. Highly secure software dots the i's and crosses the t's when it comes to requirements; that is, it has the quality of having *identified, inferred,* and *implemented* (i's) all pertinent *types* of security requirements, using *techniques* to glean those that are not quite as evident and tabulates these requirements so that they are *traceable* (t's). The team members listen to the business user and seek to understand the end-user requirements, and only then leverage this understanding to incorporate security requirements that are applicable, without losing any required functionality when translating functional specifications and governance requirements into security features. In highly secure software, there is no loss in translation of functional or assurance features.

References

Araujo, Rudolph. "Security Requirements Engineering: A Road Map." *Software Magazine,* July 2007. Web. 20 Oct. 2011. <http://www.softwaremag.com/focus-areas/security/featured-articles/security-requirements-engineering-a-road-map/>.

"Children's Online Privacy Protection Act (COPPA)." COPPA.org. Web. 20 Oct. 2011. <http://www.coppa.org/coppa.htm>.

"Comprehensive, Lightweight Application Security Process (CLASP)." Build Security In. Web. 20 Oct. 2011. <https://buildsecurityin.us-cert.gov/bsi/resources/sites/132-BSI.html>.

"ISO Standards." International Organization for Standardization (ISO). Web. 20 Oct. 2011. <http://www.iso.org/iso/iso_catalogue.htm>.

Jones, K.C. "Poor Communications, Unrealistic Scheduling Lead to IT Project Failure." *Informationweek,* 12 Mar. 2007. Web. 20 Oct. 2011. <http://www.informationweek.com/news/198000251>.

Kissel, Richard, Kevin Stine, Matthew Scholl, Hart Rossman, Jim Fahlsing, and Jessica Gulick. "Security Considerations in the System Development Life Cycle." NIST Special Publication 800-64 Revision 2, Oct. 2008. Web. 20 Oct. 2011. <http://csrc.nist.gov/publications/nistpubs/800-64-Rev2/SP800-64-Revision2.pdf>.

"NIST Standards." National Institute of Standards and Technology (NIST). Web. 20 Oct. 2011. <http://csrc.nist.gov/publications/PubsSPs.html>.

"OASIS Standards." Advancing Open Standards for the Information Society (OASIS). Web. 20 Oct. 2011. <http://www.oasis-open.org/standards>.

Opie, I. and Opie P. *The Oxford Dictionary of Nursery Rhymes.* (1951): 340–341. Print.

"Security Quality Requirements Engineering (SQUARE)." Computer Emergency Response Team (CERT). Web. 20 Oct. 2011. <http://www.cert.org/sse/square/>.

"Study of the Sarbanes-Oxley Act of 2002 Section 404 Internal Control over Financial Reporting Requirements." Securities Exchange Commission, Sept. 2009. Web. 20 Oct. 2011. <http://www.sec.gov/news/studies/2009/sox-404_study.pdf>.

"Tor Project: Overview." Tor Project: Anonymity Online. Web. 20 Oct. 2011. <https://www.torproject.org/about/overview.html.en>.

"World War 2 Poster - A Wise Old Owl Sat in an Oak." Web. 20 Oct. 2011. <http://history1900s.about.com/library/photos/blyw-wiip210.htm>.

Chapter 6

Quality #6: Is Developed Collaboratively

Two are better than one; because they have a good reward for their labor.

—*Ecclesiastes 4:9*

Prelude: There Is No "I" in Team!

Reuben, our son, and I like to play video games. The genre that we play most often is adventure games with built-in puzzles. The Lego series of games such as Indiana Jones, Batman, Star Wars, etc., is one of our favorites. These games not only have an adventurous story line true to their block-buster movie scripts, but there are many mini-games, bonus levels, and puzzles and challenges that we enjoy. Some of these challenges are quite puzzling and require careful atten-tion and thought to solve them. Reuben and I play these games together, and what I learned quickly was that when we played these games together, we were able to intelli-gently solve the puzzles in a relatively shorter time. At times, my adult brain would try to overanalyze the problem when the solution was staring right in my face, and our much-loved son would innately identify and point out; and at other times, I helped him solve some advanced and complex problems, which he did not immediately perceive. Playing solo, we would take more time to solve the problem, sometimes failing to solve the puzzle and complete the game. However, when we played together as a team, we always succeeded, leveraging each other's intelligence and aptitude.

If I may take the liberty to say so, software development is like a game; a game in which business problems must be solved and the software developer is essentially a problem solver. To intelligently and efficiently address these problems, it is important to join forces and synergize with the various stakeholders of the software. When it comes to developing secure software, it is only possible when the software is collaboratively developed, thus leveraging each party's competencies. The development team must collaborate with the many other stakeholders as they embark on developing the software.

Introduction

Quality #6 of highly secure software is that the software is collaboratively developed. Not taking into account any one of the stakeholder's interest could lead to the development of software that is relatively more susceptible to security breaches. For example, developing software purely from the business end-user's perspective and ignoring the assurance aspects can lead to vulnerable software; and taking into account the business (functional) and assurance (security) aspects of the software but not considering the legal team's interests can lead to software that is noncompliant with regulatory requirements. For the software to be secure, there must be a clear-cut understanding of the assurance aspects of the software—from the boardroom to the builder. This means that there must be synergy among the different stakeholders of the software.

Stakeholders in the Game: Whose Perspective?

Software development is complex because it has to factor in the needs of the various stakeholders who are engaged in it. One of the reasons for the increased incidences of insecure software is due to the fact that the varied perspectives of the different stakeholders are not adequately considered.

My wife, Sangeetha, and I often read Aesop's fables with our son, Reuben, to teach him values and virtues that matter. One of Aesop's fables that teaches us the importance of considering the other party's viewpoint is the story of "The Man and the Lion." For those who are unfamiliar with this fable, the story goes as follows: A man and a lion traveled together through the forest. They soon began to boast to each other of their respective superiority in strength and prowess. As they were disputing, they passed a statue carved in stone that represented "a Lion strangled by a Man." The traveler pointed to it and said: "See there! How strong we are, and how we prevail over even the king of beasts." The Lion replied: "This statue was made by one of you men. If we Lions knew how to erect statues, you would see the Man placed under the paw of the Lion." One story is good…until another is told.

This is so true when it comes to software development. Whose perspective do we take? The software development team must take into account the requirements of the following stakeholders to develop highly secure software: business, security, management, development, legal, privacy, auditors, and vendors.

Business

Needless to say, the primary stakeholder is the business, be it an external customer or an internal end user. For a while, I could start my talks about secure software development in conferences by stating that "You start coding; I will go find out what they want." This was the *modus operandi* of software development, but of late this mindset is starting to change with the inclusion of the business alongside development team members, especially in agile programming methodologies such as extreme programming or Scrum. However, it must be recognized that with the shift to programming with an agile manifesto, the speed of development and meeting sprint cycle milestones can sometimes undermine the appropriate inclusion of the business and when this is the case, security, which is commonly viewed as a nonfunctional attribute of the software gets, unfortunately, parked on the sidelines.

Irrespective of the amount of time that is allocated for the software development project, highly secure software would always factor in the business needs, not just from a functional perspective, but also from an assurance vantage point.

Security

When software is developed with security guidance in place, it is not only reliable, but also resilient and recoverable.

The software would be characterized by having the appropriate levels of controls against disclosure, alteration, and destruction threats. Data that is collected, transmitted, processed, and stored will be protected using cryptographic techniques such as encryption or hashing. Credentials will be strong against brute-force attacks and not easily guessable or crackable. Role- and resource-based access control mechanisms to protect against elevation of privilege and authorization creep will be implemented. Privileged and critical operations taken by users and processes will be tracked and auditable so that non-repudiation is assured. Data supplied by the user will be validated using whitelists (allowed values) and blacklists (disallowed values). Protection against filtration bypass using canonicalization techniques will be in place. Exceptions will not be left unhandled. Error messages will be nonverbose in nature and explicitly handled when the software errors, using the appropriate control sequences such as try-catch-finally blocks, if the programming language supports it. Session tracking variables will be unique per session and randomly generated so that it is protected against man-in-the-middle, session fixation, session hijacking, and session replay attacks. Additionally, the make-up of the software, start-up variables, and environmental configuration parameters will be protected to ensure start-up integrity and confidentiality.

Software developed with input from the security team will be characterized by having the aforementioned controls and deemed highly secure when implemented correctly.

Management

When management is engaged in the software development process, the likelihood of security controls being implemented is higher if management is cognizant and supportive of security. *Executive management* that includes the board and officers of the company hold the lion's share of responsibility when it comes to protecting the brand of the company. They are crucial in setting the direction of the company's software development processes and must be supportive of building security in. A testament to this fact is the improvement in the state of security that we see in Microsoft products. Those who have been involved in using Microsoft products must have observed a reduction in the number of the "Blue Screen of Death" (BSoD) errors and an increase in software products that are more trustworthy with features such as *Address Space Layout Randomization (ASLR)* and *Data Execution Prevention (DEP)* turned on by default. If you ask my friend, Michael Howard, author of the renowned *Writing Secure Code* book and principal cyber-security architect at Microsoft as to the spark that started the secure development mindset within Microsoft, he would invariably point you first to the memo that Microsoft founder Bill Gates sent to all the full-time employees of Microsoft and its subsidiaries. A copy of the Bill Gates trustworthy computing memo was published in the *Wired* magazine. Some pertinent and salient excerpts from that memo are given below:

> However, even more important than any of these new capabilities is the fact that it is designed from the ground up to deliver Trustworthy Computing. What I mean by this is that customers will always be able to rely on these systems to be available and to secure their information. Trustworthy Computing is computing that is as available, reliable and secure as electricity, water services and telephony.
> Our new design approaches need to dramatically reduce the number of such issues that come up in the software that Microsoft, its partners and its customers create. We need to make it automatic for customers to get the benefits of these fixes. Eventually, our software should be so fundamentally secure that customers never even worry about it.

Gates writes to focus the efforts of the company on building trust into every one of their products and services, and highlights availability, security, and privacy as the pillars of trust on which each of their software products must be built. He calls to attention the fact that flaws in even a single Microsoft product, service, or policy will not only affect the quality of their platform and services overall, but also the customer's view of Microsoft as a company. Toward the end of his memo, he concludes with

> Going forward, we must develop technologies and policies that help businesses better manage ever larger networks of PCs, servers and other intelligent devices, knowing that their critical business systems are safe from harm. Systems will have to become self-managing and inherently resilient. We need to prepare now for the kind of software that will make this happen, and we must be the kind of company that people can rely on to deliver it.

The kind of software that Bill is referring to is highly secure software. In fact, in today's computing environment, there is a vested interest for executive management to ensure that the software their company develops is secure. Failure to do so could translate the concept of "Return on Investment" (ROI) into "Risk of Incarceration." *Functional* (Development), *project,* and *program managers* are also instrumental in developing secure software when they ensure that assurance functionality is not traded off in lieu of business functionality (scope), deadlines (schedule), or budget (cost).

ROI

If security is not factored into the software that is built, "Return on Investment" can easily turn into "Risk of Incarceration" for the officers of the company.

When management collaborates with the software development team and assurance capabilities of the software are not ignored, then the resulting output will be highly secure software.

Development

In addition to programmers, the development team consists of architects, designers, testers, support, and operational personnel. It would be ideal to have a security advisor dedicated to every software development project who can guide the team to design and implement the software with trustworthy computing functionality, but pragmatically that would be close to an impossible feat. This is where the development team members can come in handy as *liaisons* of the software security initiatives with which the company must comply. It is a proven strategy to educate and train the senior members of the development staff first with what it takes to build secure software and have them act as liaisons between the development teams and the security teams. When architects and designers collaborate with the security team to design securely, not only are insecure code issues reduced, but *semantic* business logic flaws can also be potentially uncovered, even before the programmers begin to write code. When programmers collaborate with the security team to write secure code, *syntactic* bugs can be avoided. When testers collaborate with the security team, the responsibility to attest security controls is augmented using quality assurance personnel, who can be very helpful in not only validating the existence of security controls, but also their effectiveness. When the support and operations team members collaborate with the security team, they benefit from deploying and maintaining operationally hack-resilient software and not introducing any new risk into the computing ecosystem, thereby balancing the overall risk of the company.

In the creation of highly secure software, the development team members—from the coder to the configurator—play a major role.

Legal

Although it may seem like the legal team has little to do with software development, in reality the intersection that the regulatory advisors of the company have with software assurance is immense. The Sony BMG Extended Copy Protection (XCP) rootkit that installed itself automatically on customer systems when they tried to play Sony's BMG music compact discs, without soliciting consent or even notifying the user of such installation in their End User Licensing Agreement (EULA), is a good example of insufficient or lack of legal guidance when the copy protection feature was being designed and implemented. In fact, this rootkit created other vulnerabilities for malware to exploit customer systems. Sony found itself on the end of legal class-action lawsuits against them. It is therefore imperative to collaborate with the legal team if you desire to develop highly secure software.

Legal teams are extremely helpful for intellectual property (IP) protection and for the definition of detailed legalese and contractual language, as they are chartered with the responsibility of keeping the company out of harm's ways in the court of law. If you publish software, it would be foolhardy to not engage the legal team to develop the End User Licensing Agreements (EULAs), anti-reversing language, and any necessary disclaimers or "as-is" clauses. Disclaimers or "as-is" clauses serve as a risk transference mechanism, where the risk is transferred to the end user. If you publish try-before-you-buy or demo versions of the software, the legal team's guidance to specify the punitive action against violators of the terms of use must be solicited and incorporated into the installation scripts. Legal teams are also very helpful in protecting the company against copyright infringement and software piracy cases. Should your company be required to escrow the source code, then the legal team must be actively engaged in developing the escrow agreement between the related parties.

The legal team can be a powerful ally when it comes to software development as well, especially if the development is outsourced. It is crucial to establish ownership, control, and processes for the IP and technology that results from outsourced development. A clear-cut understanding of the laws of the land where the software is developed is also necessary. For example, the transfer of personal data outside Switzerland would require special permissions to be granted; and depending on the situation, if your software is transmitting data outside Switzerland, the Swiss Federal Data Protection and Information Commissioner (FDPIC) must be informed before any transfer occurs.

Additionally, control incentives, milestones, and acceptable criteria, including penalties for not meeting the requirements, must be defined using legal guidance.

Highly secure software is characterized by having legal protection mechanisms in place, which comes by collaborating with the regulatory advisors of the company.

Legalities in Software

- IP protection
- Contractual language
- Licensing (EULAs)
- Anti-Reversing
- Disclaimers
- Software piracy
- Escrow

Privacy

With the number of data protection laws and directives that your company needs to comply with, the protection of personal information cannot be ignored and the software development team must collaborate with the privacy team, if one exists. The responsibility of the Chief Privacy Officer is to ensure that personal information, be it identifiable (PII), health (PHI), or financial (PFI), is protected against unauthorized disclosure. When software collects, processes, transmits, and/or stores such personal information, it is imperative for the software to assure confidentiality of that information.

Highly secure software will factor in the privacy requirements and ensure that the requirements of the privacy stakeholder are satisfied.

Auditors

An information security audit is a technical, systematic, and measurable evaluation of how the security policies have been implemented within a company. It must be recognized that the security audit is not a one-time event, but an ongoing process that can assist in the definition and maintenance of contextually current and correct information security policies. Some forms of evaluation include interviews, vulnerability scans, analysis of operating systems security settings, minimum security baselines analysis, review of credential protection configuration settings, review of network configuration settings, logging and auditing review, backup and recovery assurance, documentation evidence, and historical data analysis.

Audit evaluations require the collection and submission of information that demonstrates the evidence of controls. Before the external auditors arrive on site to conduct an audit, the internal auditors can use previous audits to determine the information that will be required. Some examples include

- The strength and complexity of credentials (e.g., passwords, tokens, etc.)
- Authorization rules and Access Control Lists (ACLs)
- Information being logged and access to log files
- Operating systems patch levels
- Minimum security baseline configurations
- Backup data, location, recovery objectives, and plan
- Cryptographic protection, agility, key management, and configurations

- Documentation of configuration and code changes
- Evidence of secure development processes such as threat models, code reviews, security testing, and secure deployment

Pre-knowledge of the kind of information that the auditors will require can be useful in designing the software so that it can provide such information with ease, when solicited during an information security audit. This is particularly true when it comes to the auditing functionality of the software. Knowing what the auditors would want and logging that information with the appropriate level of verbosity in the audit logs makes the collection of audit information easy. It is, however, crucial to present the information to the auditors as is, without massaging it to pass an audit, and so this must be a controlled activity conducted by individuals who are authorized and have a need to know.

Highly secure software is characterized by having been developed after the development team has collaborated with the internal auditors to address audit requirements.

Vendors

One may wonder as to what vendors have to do with highly secure software. The software computing ecosystem is predominantly a mixture of custom-built in-house applications, third-party commercial/government off-the-shelf (COTS/GOTS), and in some cases merely a subscription to the Software as a Service (SaaS).

Engaging the vendors is critical in ensuring that the computing ecosystem is secure. Communicating security requirements to third-party COTS software and GOTS software vendors and attesting their claims of security features is vital to assure the resiliency of the software being procured.

In cloud computing delivery models, such as Platform as a Service (PaaS), Infrastructure as a Service (IaaS), or Software as a Service (SaaS), a thorough understanding of the application programming interfaces (APIs) is necessary so that the security of the data and systems is certain. The same is also true of mobile APIs. In the "Top Threats to Cloud Computing" publication, the Cloud Security Alliance lists insecure interfaces and API as one of the top two threats, second only to the abuse and nefarious use of cloud computing. Cloud and mobile computing APIs are used to build applications and software that operate in the cloud or on mobile devices. These APIs expose the functionality provided by the service provider and provisioning, management, orchestration, and monitoring are all provided using these interfaces. The APIs create a single point of failure in a cloud solution because the security and availability of general services depend on the security of these APIs. Without proper authentication and access control, these APIs can be subject to unauthorized discovery and invocation. Without proper cryptographic protection when leveraging these APIs, sensitive information and credentials can be exposed. It is also crucially important to understand the dependency chain with the API.

When software vendors are actively engaged and security requirements are communicated and attested in procured software, and/or one understands and implements controls to mitigate the security threats, the resulting software would be highly secure.

Insecure Interfaces

Vendor APIs should be reviewed from a security perspective because they can become the single point of failure if they are insecure or porous.

Figure 6.1 depicts the various stakeholders that are involved in a software development project.

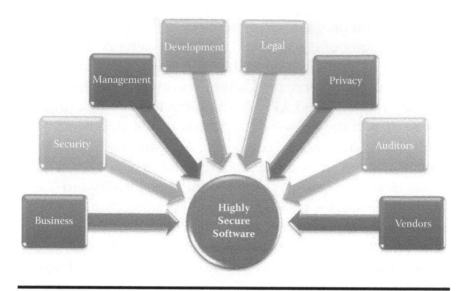

Figure 6.1   Secure software development stakeholders.

Conclusion

Quality #6 of highly secure software is that the software is collaboratively developed, factoring in the considerations and requirements of the various stakeholders. Why? Because with collaboration comes synergy and strength. The sagacious adage, "United we stand, divided we fall," aptly fits this quality of highly secure software. This phrase has been used many times to garner support in independence struggles and is attributed to Aesop for one of his fables known as "The Bundle of Sticks." In this fable, a dying old man teaches his children that they can easily break each stick in a bundle when it is separated, but when the sticks are put together in a bundle, then the act of breaking the sticks in the bundle is an impossible feat. In like manner, when the stakeholders of a software development project collaborate, then one can leverage the intelligence and aptitude of each stakeholder (business, security, management, development, legal, privacy, auditors, and vendor) and synergistically develop hacker-resilient software that is not easily breakable. In this way, not only can they solve the business problem in the game of software development, but they can do so in a highly secure manner.

United We Stand

United we stand, divided we fall, for with collaboration comes synergy and strength.

References

"Bill Gates: Trustworthy Computing." *Wired.com*, 17 Jan. 2002. Web. 20 Oct. 2011. <http://www.wired.com/techbiz/media/news/2002/01/49826>.

"Federal Data Protection and Information Commissioner (FDPIC)." Der Eidgenössische Datenschutz- Und Öffentlichkeitsbeauftragte (EDÖB). Web. 20 Oct. 2011. <http://www.edoeb.admin.ch/org/00447/index.html?lang=en>.

Hayes, Bill. "Conducting a Security Audit: An Introductory Overview." Symantec Connect Community, 02 Nov. 2010. Web. 20 Oct. 2011. <http://www.symantec.com/connect/articles/conducting-security-audit-introductory-overview>.

Kissel, Richard, Kevin Stine, Matthew Scholl, Hart Rossman, Jim Fahlsing, and Jessica Gulick. "Security Considerations in the System Development Life Cycle." NIST Special Publication 800-64 Revision 2, Oct. 2008. Web. 20 Oct. 2011. <http://csrc.nist.gov/publications/nistpubs/800-64-Rev2/SP800-64-Revision2.pdf>.

Patel, Rajiv P. and Ralph M. Pais. "Software Outsourcing — Business and Legal Issues Checklist." Fenwick & West LLC. Web. 20 Oct. 2011. <http://www.fenwick.com/docstore/publications/ip/ip_articles/outsourcing_offshore.pdf>.

Peterson, Gunnar. "Security Architecture Blueprint." Arctec Group, LLC, 2007. Web. 20 Oct. 2011. <http://arctecgroup.net/pdf/ArctecSecurityArchitectureBlueprint.pdf>.

Posey, Brien M. "Demystifying the 'Blue Screen of Death'"
TechRepublic. Microsoft TechNet. Web. 20 Oct. 2011.
<http://technet.microsoft.com/en-us/library/cc750081.aspx>.
Russinovich, Mark. "Sony, Rootkits and Digital Rights Management
Gone Too Far." TechNet Blogs, 31 Oct. 2005. Web. 20
Oct. 2011. <http://blogs.technet.com/b/markrussinovich/
archive/2005/10/31/sony-rootkits-and-digital-rights-manage-
ment-gone-too-far.aspx>.
Silver, Judith. "Software Legalities Part 2 — Software Escrow »
SitePoint." SitePoint, 27 May 2002. Web. 20 Oct. 2011. <http://
www.sitepoint.com/legalities-2-software-escrow/>.
"Top Threats to Cloud Computing V1.0." Cloud Security Alliance
(CSA), Mar. 2010. Web. 20 Oct. 2011. <https://cloudsecurity-
alliance.org/topthreats/csathreats.v1.0.pdf>.

Chapter 7

Quality #7: Is Adaptable

... this one thing I do, forgetting those things which
are behind, and reaching forth unto those things
which are before, I press toward the mark for the
prize of the high calling ...

—Philippians 3:13-14

Prelude: The Shark is a Polyphyodont

My wife and I started our careers as shark researchers in the
Bimini Islands situated in the commonwealth of the Bahamas.
Our research work focused on the breeding and navigational
behaviors of lemon sharks *(Negaprion brevirostris)*. During our
time of research, we learned a lot of interesting facts about
sharks. For example, sharks need to keep on swimming to
stay alive, sharks cannot swim backward, and sharks—like
most toothed fishes—are polyphyodonts. A polyphyodont is
an organism whose teeth are continuously being replaced. In
fact, in the case of sharks, the teeth are modified placoid der-
mal scales, and the older rows of teeth are replaced by newer
ones continuously throughout the life of the shark.

In a similar manner, when it comes to secure software, the software must be continuously renewing its armor, throughout its life, against hacker threats.

Introduction

Quality #7 of highly secure software is that the software is adaptable. This means that the software is architected and implemented in such a manner that it is flexible to address future changes to computing architecture, methodologies, and threats. That is, the software is developed with a strategic and holistic perspective, and it will be *continuously improved* to address any changes that can happen in the future.

Law of Resiliency Degradation

In a room filled with a hundred people, if I was to ask, how many of you have software in your companies that was developed 3 to 5 years ago, it is likely that more than 50 percent of that group is going to respond affirmatively. We often refer to this aged software as legacy software. Now if I were to ask about the security features in that legacy software, chances are that, of the people who responded affirmatively to my first question, only a handful would also answer my second question accurately and affirmatively. The truth is that most legacy software was designed with mere functionality in mind, and the assurance aspects of the software were not part of the equation when it was developed. But unlike the vestigial appendix in the human body that is believed to serve no function, legacy software still serves some functional use to the company. However, just as the vestigial appendix organ is susceptible to appendicitis infections, thence requiring surgical removal, legacy software can be susceptible to changing threats and may require secure disposal.

Vestigial Software

Just as the appendix organ is susceptible to appendicitis infections thence requiring surgical removal, legacy software is susceptible to changing threats and so it requires secure disposal.

Having said that, the question now changes as to whether the software is resilient against hacker attacks in today's computing environment. To determine this, it is important for us to understand a phenomenon that I like to call the "law of resiliency degradation."

The Law of Resiliency Degradation

Over time, the ability of the software to withstand attacks wanes, due to changes in technologies, threats, and the talent pool.

The law of resiliency degradation is the condition that over time, software that is considered secure—meaning its resiliency levels are above the acceptable risk levels—loses its ability to withstand attacks. This degradation happens because of various changes in the computing ecosystem, ranging from changes in technologies, to threats, and even the talent pool. And as the effectiveness of the implemented controls decrease and the resiliency of the software wanes, at one point in time it will meet the acceptable risk level, which is the *point of risk avoidance.* The point of risk avoidance is the time when the software must be replaced by another, which is more resilient or with the next version of the software that has increased resiliency above the acceptable risk levels. Failure to have a plan to end the insecure version of the software

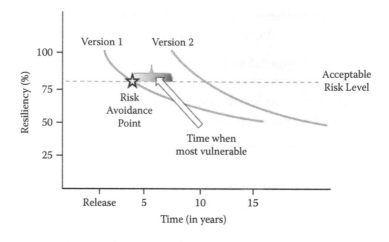

Figure 7.1   Law of resiliency degradation.

before it reaches the risk avoidance point is unwise because each moment that the software continues to operate past the point of risk avoidance leaves the software most vulnerable to attack. Figure 7.1 depicts this phenomenon.

Software Adaptability: Technology, Threats, and Talent

The changes that the software must be adaptable to can be primarily classified into the following three types of changes: technology, threats, and talent.

Technology

The world of software is not static. In fact, it could be argued that software development is extremely dynamic and fast changing. From the punch cards to the monolithic self-contained applications that run on the mainframe, to distributing computing software, Rich Internet Applications (RIA), and Software as a Service (SaaS), we have observed that not only has the methodology of software development changed, but the technologies involved in software development have also changed.

For example, a technological change that best explains the need for software to be adaptable, to stay secure, is described below. Not too long ago, software that used the MD5 hashing function for cryptographic protection was considered secure. But today the MD5 hashing function is proven to be *collision* prone, meaning that two different inputs can result in the same output hash. This renders the software susceptible to spoofing and brute-force attacks. It is therefore imperative for the software to be flexible to adapt efficiently to upcoming technological changes and to continue to assure trust. In our scenario, this means, that the software is architected with *cryptographic agility*, meaning that it is easy for us to switch algorithms and replace the MD5 hashing function with a more secure cryptographic algorithm that is relatively less susceptible to today's threats.

For the software to be resilient with changing technologies, the software must be architected to be flexible and adaptable. The software development methodology itself plays a major part to provide such adaptability. Traditional waterfall methodology that is characterized by a structured and linear development process with definitive phases is not very conducive to developing adaptable software. To address this challenge, other software development methodologies, such as prototyping and rapid application development (RAD), are used. One of these RAD methodologies is the Adaptive Software Development (ASD) methodology that embodies the principle of continuous process improvement. The ASD process has a repeating series of speculate, collaborate, and learning cycles that is dynamic in nature. This allows for continuous learning and adaptation to the emerging states of the software and environment. But for some reason the ASD did not gain as much traction as did the very similar and prevalent agile development methodology. Extreme programming and Scrum are examples of agile software development methodologies. They are based on iterative and incremental development. Not only do the requirements but also the solutions evolve over time through collaboration. Agile software development stimulates adaptive planning, evolutionary development and delivery, time-boxed iterations, and encourages rapid and flexible response to change as expressed in the Agile manifesto specified in Figure 7.2. Agile software development methodologies are therefore more adept at addressing changing requirements and computing environment landscapes. This can be leveraged in developing software that is adaptable and highly secure.

To Be or Not To Be Agile?

Agile software development stimulates adaptive planning, evolutionary development and delivery, time-boxed iterations, and encourages rapid and flexible response to change, making it relatively more adept in developing adaptable secure software.

In addition to the software development methodology itself, the architecture of the software plays a major role in the adaptability of the software. Software architects and designers must look at the software they design from a strategic (long-term) perspective. Software should be designed to be

We are uncovering better ways of developing software by doing it and helping others do it. Through this work, we have come to value:

1. Individuals and interactions over processes and tools.

2. Working software over comprehensive documentation.

3. Customer collaboration over contractual negotiation.

4. Responding to change over following a plan.

Figure 7.2 Manifesto for agile software development.

useful until the identified end-of-life (EOL), in addition to addressing the business problem in the immediate time frame. For software to be adaptable, it should be highly *cohesive* in nature, meaning that the functionality of the software must be broken down into units that are discrete in their functions. Additionally, the software must be architected so that it is *loosely coupled.* This means that the dependencies between related modules of the software are weak, and so switching out modules with alternatives, particularly insecure ones with safer ones, is relatively easier. Highly secure software is developed using methodologies that make it easy to adapt to changing trends and is characterized by being *highly cohesive* and *loosely coupled.*

Threats

In addition, the threat landscape has also been changing. Network attacks are giving way to more application or software attacks and, as aforementioned in one of the earlier qualities, the attackers' motivations are changing and different as well.

Hackers are generally characterized by a few personality traits, three of which are mentioned. One trait of hackers is that they are *extremely creative,* and when you try to sandbox them, they try to find a way to get out of the sandbox by circumventing the controls that are in place. The second trait of hackers is that they *seek out the path of least resistance.* You may be familiar with the story of the two friends who were hiking in a jungle. They were confronted by a bear in the woods. One of the friends reached into his backpack and pulled out and put on a pair of running shoes. Upon seeing this, the other friend questioned him, "Do you really think that you can run faster than the bear with those shoes?", to which the one wearing the shoes replied, "I don't have to run faster than the bear, I just have to run faster than you." In like manner, if your company's software is weaker than your competitor's, it is more likely that hackers will target your applications and software over your competitor's. Your software should be agile in its defense against threat agents. The third trait of hackers is that they *adapt quickly to the changing landscape.* This is evident from the kinds of threats that we can observe in today's computing world. As the adoption of mobile computing technologies increases, the types of threats that are observed seem to be targeting these devices and platforms. MSNBC's report in its Security section that Google had to pull out more than fifty apps from the Android Market, because they contained malware that could compromise sensitive and personal data of the owners of the Android devices, is a testament to the fact that the threat landscape is changing from online fraud to the mobile field.

Hacker Traits

1. Extremely creative
2. Seek the path of least resistance
3. Very adaptive

We also observe this in nature. When a particular waterhole dries up, you observe that the predators move to the next waterhole where the prey would congregate to quench their thirst. So as hackers move on to newer landscapes, we must equally adapt as well. Just as it is essential for us to breathe to live, it is equally essential for our software to be adaptable to changing threats or else it will get hacked.

Highly secure software, when developed, takes into account these changing threats. *SC Magazine,* in its article titled "How did software security change with evolving malware threats" refers to Stuxnet as intelligent malware, and highlights the need for security software to adapt and that the future of the software comes down to its flexibility to address changing threats. This is very true. In a few decades from now, I predict that the software that will survive and continue to serve its business is the software that is currently being designed and implemented to tackle both current and future threats. This means that the software is built with a security mindset that is both *tactical* and *strategic*. For example, if you determine that the software is susceptible to buffer overflow attacks, it would be important to not only patch the software and address the security vulnerability with bounds checking and input size/length validation, but also to have an implementable plan in place to replace banned or deprecated APIs with safer alternatives or use managed code programming languages that are less susceptible to overflow attacks. In other words, highly secure software is not only about patch management, but also problem management. Patch management is necessary, and security hot-fixes and patches are essential to contain the exposure upon incidents, but problem management aims to determine the root cause and eliminate the vulnerabilities for good. Root cause analysis gives insight into "why" the security threat is even possible, and pulling the problem out by its roots creates sustainable and secure software.

Incident or Problem Management

Eliminate the problem from its root; don't just patch it!

Talent

With looming opportunities and plummeting employer-to-employee loyalties, there is an increase in the number of talented people moving from one company to another. What is often overlooked is that with the move, a lot of business and functional knowledge walks out the door as well. Irrespective of the size of the company, all companies need to pay attention to this problem for it is speculated that in the future, there will be a dearth of talented workers. The *McKinsey Quarterly* reported that the war for talent has not ended, and it is imperative for companies to make their talent (workforce) a strategic priority.

Although it may not be so obvious, this shift in and lack of talented workforces directly translates into the secure state of the software that the company develops. In fact, the strongest security asset inside a company is its people, but the caveat is that they can also be the weakest link. Legal instruments such as nondisclosure agreements and noncompete agreements, wherever applicable and enforceable, can be useful to limit the disclosure of intellectual property, when people move around. Highly secure software is characterized by being developed by people who have agreed to abide by these legal protection mechanisms.

The adaptability of highly secure software to talent pool changes is also related to how the software was architected. A humorous yet very pertinent article that I would point your attention to is titled "How to write unmaintainable code" and ensure a job for life. Interestingly, however, an inverse of what the article suggests would, in fact, generate not only maintainable code, but also secure code. For example, the article prescribes to never validate and avoid encapsulation in the interest of efficiency and, when this is not followed, the output is software that is less susceptible to overflow attacks or insecure direct object reference attacks. The article also suggests ignoring standard libraries and rolling out your own custom-developed implementations. When this is the case, the software is no longer flexible to change and hence less adaptable.

Highly secure software is characterized by having used proven and vetted standards and libraries, so that when there is another standard that is mandated or a safer library, it is relatively easier to switch out the outgoing standard or unsafe library for the new or safe one. One of the important things that must be checked for during secure code reviews is the use of deprecated/banned APIs and standards in code. For example, C code that uses strcpy or strncpy for copying string data into memory buffers is replaced with strcpy_s calls in highly secure software—until a replacement for strcpy_s is necessary. Similarly, the Data Encryption Standard (DES) as the standard for cryptographic algorithms should be replaced with more secure standards such as the Advanced Encryption Standard (AES). When standards are used in the creation of software, it reduces the coupling of the software code to the people who wrote it; and when people move around, the software is still maintainable and relatively easier to fix and adapt to the changes in talent.

Being Predictive

A good hockey player plays where the puck is. A great hockey player plays where the puck is going to be.

Wayne "The Great One" Gretzky
Professional hockey player

Begin with the Future in Mind

We started the qualities of highly secure software by stating that we must be proactive in building security in, and map it to a plan, beginning with the end in mind; but highly secure software is not only about being proactive, but *predictive* as well. We must anticipate the unexpected and begin by building our software with the future in mind. President Abraham Lincoln said, "The best way to predict the future is to create it" and in the context of software security, it is no different. Software that you create today with the flexibility to adapt and change to mitigate future threats can assure your company's future.

Secure Software Requires Security-Savvy People

To develop highly secure software that is predictive in nature, your company needs to invest in having the right people do the right things at the right time. That is, your people must be security savvy when building software. Security-savvy-people are those who are aware, trained, and educated in building hacker-resilient software. To be *aware* means that the person knows what controls must be built into the software. To be *trained* means that the person has the appropriate skills to design, implement, deploy, and attest to the software's ability to withstand attacks. To be *educated* means that the person is learned and capable of making calculated decisions regarding the security of the software. Whether a company's people are the strongest defense or the weakest link is directly proportional to the effectiveness of the security awareness, training, and education programs within the company.

Security Savvy

Security-savvy people are those who are aware, trained, and educated in building highly secure, hacker-resilient software.

In addition to being aware, trained, and educated, people proficient in software security also display the trait of being adaptable themselves. Not only are they well versed in content knowledge regarding software security threats and have effective communication skills, but they also stay current with newer threats and adapt quickly to mitigating these threats. Highly secure software is characterized by being developed by people who are highly security minded.

Conclusion

Quality #7 of highly secure software is that the software is adaptable. Because the ability of the software to withstand attacks reduces over time, it is important for the software to be continuously renewing its armor to stay in business. This requires anticipating the future and investing in making the people within your company security savvy so that they can create highly secure software. Benjamin Franklin is attributed to have said, "Without continual growth and progress, such words as improvement, achievement, and success have no meaning," and he could not be more accurate. The software must be architected in such a manner that it can quickly adapt to changes in technology, threats, and talent. Without such adaptability, it is only a matter of time before the software designed, developed, and deployed can come back to bite you when it gets hacked.

References

Chansanchai, Athima. "Malware Infects More than 50 Android Apps." MSNBC.com, 2 Mar. 2011. Web. 20 Oct. 2011. <http:// www.msnbc. msn.co m/id/41867328/ns/technology_and_science -security/>.

"Cyber Criminals Adapt As Threat Landscape Changes." Cyveillance Blog — The Latest Cyber Intelligence Information on Identity Theft, Phishing, Malware and Fraud. Web. 20 Oct. 2011. <http://www.cyveillan ceblog.com/general-cyberintel /cyber-cri minals-adapt-as-threat- landscape-changes>.

Guthridge, Matthew, Asmus B. Komm, and Emily Lawson. "Making Talent a Strategic Priority." *The McKinsey Quarterly,* 2008. Web. 20 Oct. 2011. <http://www managingpeoplebook.com/ WarForTalentNeverEnded.pdf>.

Hamlett, William C. *Sharks, Skates, and Rays: the Biology of Elasmobranch Fishes.* Baltimore: Johns Hopkins UP, 1999. 58. Print.

Highsmith, James A. *Adaptive Software Development: A Collaborative Approach to Managing Complex Systems.* New York: Dorset House Pub., 2000. Print.

Highsmith, Jim. "Messy, Exciting, and Anxiety-Ridden: Adaptive Software Development." *American Programmer* X.1 (1997). Jan. 1997. Web. 20 Oct. 2011. <http://www.adaptivesd.com/articles/messy.htm>.

Hunter, Amy. "How Your Appendix Works." HowStuffWorks. Web. 20 Oct. 2011. <http://science.howstuffw orks.com/environmental/ life/human-biology/ap pendix.htm>.

Leyden, John. "Weak Sigs Found on One in Seven SSL Sites." *The Register,* 7 Jan. 2009. Web. 20 Oct. 2011. <http://www.thereg ister.co.uk/2009/01/07/ssl_security_survey/>.

Manifesto for Agile Software Development. Web. 20 Oct. 2011. <http://www.agilemanifesto.org/>.

Raywood, Dan. "How Did Security Software Change with the Evolving Malware Threat in 2010 and Where Will It Go in 2011?" *SC Magazine UK,* 06 Dec. 2010. Web. 20 Oct. 2011. <http://www.scmagazineu k.com/how-did-security-software-change-with-the- evolving-mal ware-threat-in-2010-and-whe re-will-it-go-in-2011/a rticle/192228/>.

"Security-Savvy Workforce: Designing a Security Awareness Program That Works." *Talent Management Magazine.* Web. 20 Oct. 2011. <http://talentmgt.com/articles /view/securitysavvy_workforce_designing_a_security_awareness_program_ that_works/4>.

Chapter 8

Epilogue

We started our journey, regarding the seven qualities of highly secure software, learning that Quality #1 is about building security in by being proactive. Quality #2 is about beginning with the end in mind, meaning that we plan for the security controls that are to be built into the software, and that the controls implemented and deployed map to a security plan. Quality #3 is about putting first things first and incorporating the foundational elements of highly secure software, which includes protection against disclosure, alteration, destruction or denial-of-service, and assurance of authentication, authorization, and auditing. Quality #4 highlights the need to think win-win by balancing risk with reward, functionality with assurance, and threats with appropriate controls that mitigate those threats. Quality #5 brings to our attention the need for the security team to understand what the business requirements are before they incorporate security requirements into the software they build. Quality #6 brings to light that highly secure software is not developed in a silo, but is collaboratively developed, taking into account the synergies among the varied stakeholders. Finally, we learn that Quality #7 is about continuously improving the state of security in the software

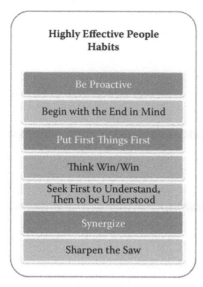
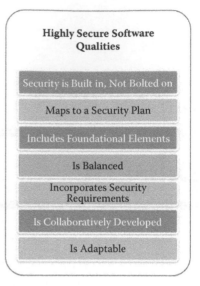

Figure 8.1   Parallelism between the "highly effective people habits" and "highly secure software qualities."

by designing it to be adaptable to changes in technologies, threats, and talent pool.

Figure 8.1 indicates that parallelism between the seven qualities of highly secure software and the seven habits of highly effective people.

In conclusion, when growing up, I was taught that the way something becomes a habit is that it starts out with "IT" (whatever "it" is), and then it becomes a "BIT" to "A-BIT" of your life, until it finally becomes a "H-ABIT." In likewise manner, to build highly secure software, I reckon that you start with one or two qualities of highly secure software until you get to have all the qualities ingrained into your company's software development life cycle.

I trust that you enjoyed reading this book as much as I enjoyed writing it. Until we connect next time, let us go forth and build highly secure software.

Index

Page numbers followed by f
indicate figure
Page numbers followed by t
indicate table

A

Abuse case modeling, 96, 97f
Access Control Lists (ACLs), 113
ACLs. *See* Access Control Lists
(ACLs)
Adaptive Software Development
(ASD), 123
Address Space Layout
Randomization (ASLR), 108
Advanced Encryption Standard
(AES), 129
Adware, 40
AES. *See* Advanced Encryption
Standard (AES)
Agile software development, 124,
124f
American Public Broadcasting
Service (PBS), 24
"An Inquiry into the Nature and
Causes of the Wealth of
Nations " (Smith), 18
Anonymity, 93, 94
"Anonymous edition", 22–23
APIs. *See* Application programming
interfaces (APIs)

Applicable controls identification, in
security plan development,
40–41
Applicable requirements
identification, in security
plan development, 40
Application programming interfaces
(APIs), 115
*Application Security: 2011 and
Beyond,* 25
Application Vulnerability
Description Language
(AVDL), 93
Art of War, 40
ASD. *See* Adaptive Software
Development (ASD)
ASLR. *See* Address Space Layout
Randomization (ASLR)
Assurance
integrity, 59, 61
software, 27–28, 27f
Assuring Privacy, 94
Attacks
denial-of-service, 85t
firewalls and, 6
information disclosure, 85t
insiders, 6
intrusion detection systems/
intrusion prevention
systems and, 12
malicious file execution, 85t

man-in-the-middle, 9, 59, 83t
phishing and social engineering,
    22
repudiation, 85t
session, 83t
Audit, information security, 113
Auditing, 68–69, 70t
Auditing and Accountability, 44
Auditors, 113–114
Authentication, 70t
Authentication attacks, 83t
Authorization creep, 67–68
Availability, 62–68, 70t
Availability objectives, in security
    plan development, 39, 39f
AVDL. *See* Application Vulnerability
    Description Language
    (AVDL)

B

BAIT. *See* Business Aware
    Information Technology
    (BAIT)
"Balancing Act: Security
    Vs. Functionality"
    (GovInfoSecurity.com), 77
Balancing scale
    functionality and assurance,
        77–8, 88–89
    risk and reward, 74–77, 76t
    threats and controls, 80–82
BASS. *See* Business Aware Secure
    Software (BASS)
Bejtlich, Richard, 20
Bertocci, Vittorio, 10
"Big data: The next frontier for
    innovation, competition,
    and productivity"
    (McKinsey & Company), 52
Blackhat USA conference, 2009, 10
Blacklist filters, 13

"Blue Screen of Death" (BSoD)
    errors, 108
Boardroom objectives, 75–77, 76t
Boundaries, computing
    environment and, 6
Brand savings, 20
Browser, 9
Browser Exploits against SSL/TLS
    (BEAST), 12–14
Brute-force attacks, 84t
BSoD errors. *See* "Blue Screen of
    Death" (BSoD) errors
Buffer, 83t
Buffer overflow, 127
Business, software development
    and, 106, 116f
Business Aware Information
    Technology (BAIT), 95
Business Aware Secure Software
    (BASS), 95
Business functionality, internally
    mandated security
    requirements and, 94–95
Bypass, 83t

C

CA. *See* Certificate authority (CA)
C & A. *See* Certification and
    accreditation (C&A)
Cache, protecting information in, 57
California civil code 1798.82. *See*
    State Bill 1386
Canadian Personal Information
    Protection and Electronic
    Documents Act (PIPEDA),
    91
Canonicalization attacks, 13
Canonicalization techniques, 107
Certificate authority (CA), 9
Certification and accreditation
    (C&A), 42–43

Chabrow, Eric, 77
Children's Online Privacy
        Protection Act (COPPA), 93
CLASP. *See* Comprehensive,
        Lightweight Application
        Security Process (CLASP)
Cleartext, 56
Cloud computing, 6
Cloud Security Alliance, 115
Code signing, 61
Commercial/government off-the-
        shelf (COTS/GOTS), 114
Company policies and standards,
        internally mandated security
        requirements and, 94
Comprehensive, Lightweight
        Application Security
        Process (CLASP), 97, 99
Computing environment, 6
Confidentiality, 54–58, 70t
Confidentiality assurance, 55
Confidentiality objectives, in
        security plan development,
        39, 39f, 41
Configuration control mechanism,
        26
COPPA. *See* Children's Online
        Privacy Protection Act
        (COPPA)
Cost, 79
COTS/GOTS. *See* Commercial/
        government off-the-shelf
        (COTS/GOTS)
Covert secret writing technique, 55
Criminal hacking, 22
Cross-site request forgery (CSRF), 84t
Cross-Site Scripting (XSS) attacks,
        12, 13, 19, 82, 83t
cryptographic agility, 123
Cryptography, 55
CSRF. *See* Cross-site request forgery
        (CSRF)

D

"Dangers without, Dangers within:
        Network security in the
        age of e-commerce"
        (Salgado, Jr.), 10
Data, importance of, 51–53
Data breaches, 20
Data classification, 96, 97f
Data Encryption Standard (DES), 129
Data Execution Prevention (DEP),
        108
Data integrity, 61
Data loss (or leakage) prevention
        (DLP), 7
de Bracton Henry, 15
Decryption, 56
Denial-of service (DoS), 7, 14, 53, 85t
DEP. *See* Data Execution Prevention
        (DEP)
DES. *See* Data Encryption Standard
        (DES)
Design phase, in building security, 26
Development, in building security, 26
Digital assets, 51
Disclosure threats, 55
Distributed DoS (DDoS) tool, 24
DLP. *See* Data loss (or leakage)
        prevention (DLP)
Duong, Thai, 12

E

Egorenkov, Alexander, 23
Electronic Business, 10
Encrypted web.config file, 58f
Encryption, 55, 56
End-to-end security, 10
End User Licensing Agreement
        (EULA), 111
EULA. *See* End User Licensing
        Agreement (EULA)

European Union (EU) Data
Protection Directive, 91
Executive management, 107
"Exploits of a Mom", 62
Extended Copy Protection (XCP), 111
eXtensible Access Control Markup
Language (XACML), 93
Externally imposed security
requirements, 89–94, 90f

F

Fail closed, 63
Fail open, 63
Farrow, Rik, 10
FBI. *See* Federal Bureau of
Investigation (FBI)
FDPIC. *See* Swiss Federal Data
Protection and Information
Commissioner (FDPIC)
Fear, uncertainty, and doubt (FUD),
16
Federal Bureau of Investigation
(FBI), 10
Federal Information Security
Management Act (FISMA), 91
Firewall, 3
attacks inside, 7–8
implementing, 4–8
network, 6, 7
Firewall administrator, 4
FISMA. *See* Federal Information
Security Management Act
(FISMA)
Forrester Forrsights Security Survey, 25
Foundational assurance elements,
51, 54–69, 70t
FUD. *See* Fear, uncertainty, and
doubt (FUD)
Full disclosure, 20
Functionality and assurance, in
balancing scale, 77–80,
88–89

G

Gartner Group, 5
Gates, Bill, 108–109
Geekonomics (Rice), 21
GeoHot. *See* Hotz, George
George, Richard "Dickie", 77
GLBA. *See* Gramm-Leach-Bliley Act
(GLBA)
Global economy, data and, 52
Globalization, 21
GovInfoSecurity.com, 77
Graf_Chokolo. *See* Egorenkov,
Alexander
Gramm-Leach-Bliley Act (GLBA),
40, 91
Gretzky, Wayne, 129

H

Hacker group, 24
The Hacker News, 22
Hackers
personality traits of, 125–126
security landscape and, 22
three C's motivating, 24
Hacking, 20, 22
Harvard Business Review, 22
Hash calc values, 56, 60f
Hash functions, 61
Hashing, 55, 56, 59
Hashing control, 45
Hash sum, 56
Health Insurance Portability and
Accountability Act (HIPAA),
91
HIDS and NIDS. *See* Host and
network IDSs (HIDS and
NIDS)
Hijacking, session, 83t
HIPAA. *See* Health Insurance
Portability and
Accountability Act (HIPAA)

Host and network IDSs (HIDS and NIDS), 14
Hotz, George, 23
Howard, Michael, 108
HTTP. *See* HyperText Transport Protocol (HTTP)
Hyneman, Jamie, 3
HyperText Transport Protocol (HTTP), 10, 11

I

IaaS. *See* Infrastructure as a Service (IaaS)
IDSs. *See* Intrusion DetectionSystems (IDSs)
Industry standards, 92
Information disclosure, sources of, 57
Information disclosure attacks, 85t
Information security audit, 113
Infrastructure as a Service (IaaS), 17, 115
Injection flaws, 83t
Input validation, 61
Insecure cryptographic storage, 84t
Insecure direct object reference, 84t
Insecure Interfaces, 115
Insecure software, 21
Insider attacks, 6
Integer overflow, 83t
Integrity 58–62, 60f, 70t
referential, 61
Integrity assurance, 59, 61
Integrity objectives, in security plan development, 39
Intellectual property (IP) protection, legal teams and, 111
Internally imposed security requirements, 89–91, 90f, 94
Internal systems attacks, 6

International Organization for Standardization (ISO), 92
Intrusion Detection Systems (IDSs), 3, 4, 12–14
Intrusion Prevention Systems (IPSs), 3, 4, 12–14
IPSs. *See* Intrusion Prevention Systems (IPSs)
Iron triangle, 78, 78f, 79
ISO. *See* International Organization for Standardization (ISO)
ISO 27000 series (Information Security Management Systems), 92

K

Key Management Interoperability Protocol Specification, 93

L

Law of resiliency degradation, 120–122, 122f
Legal teams, software development and, 111–112
Logging control, 44, 45
Lulzec (Hacker group), 24

M

Malicious file execution attacks, 85t
Management, software development and, 107–110, 116f
Management controls, 38, 41
Man-in-the-middle (MITM) attacks, 9, 59, 83t
Manning, Bradley, 24
Mapped software, 44–46
Marlinspike, Moxie, 10
Marshalls, 53
Massachusetts 201 CMR 17.00, 91
McKinsey & Company, 52

McKinsey Quarterly, 127
MD5 hashing function, 123
Means, building security and, 24–27
Message digest, 56
Microsoft products, 107, 109
Microsoft TechNet, 15
Misuse cases. *See* Abuse case
    modeling
MITM attacks. *See* Man-in-the-
    middle (MITM) attacks
Motives, building security and, 24–27
MSNBC's (Security section report), 126
Multi-factor authentication, 65
Mythbusters (TV Show), 3

N

National Institute of Standards and
    Technology (NIST), 41, 92
National Security Agency (NSA), 77
"Need-to-know" principle, 67
Network architecture manager, 4
Network firewalls, 6, 7
Network flooding, 14
Network security firewall
    administrator, 5
Network security professional, 4, 5
NIST. *See* National Institute of
    Standards and Technology
    (NIST)
Non-human threats, 40
Normalization of logs, 14
NSA. *See* National Security Agency
    (NSA)

O

OASIS. *See* Organization for the
    Advancement of Structured
    Information Standards
    (OASIS)
On-demand, pay-per-use
    subscription model, 6

The Onion Routing, 93
Open source tools, 10
Operational controls, 38
Opportunity, building security and,
    24–27
Organization for the Advancement
    of Structured Information
    Standards (OASIS), 92
Overflow threats, 83t
Overt secret writing technique, 55

P

PaaS. *See* Platform as a Service
    (PaaS)
Payment Card Industry Data
    Security Standard (PCI
    DSS), 36, 40, 45, 92, 94
PBS. *See* American Public
    Broadcasting Service (PBS)
PCI DSS. *See* Payment Card
    Industry Data Security
    Standard (PCI DSS)
People, process, and technology,
    Software security and, 21
Personal health information (PHI),
    91
Personally identifiable information
    (PII), 93
Petronas Twin Towers, 50
PHI. *See* Personal health
    information (PHI)
PII. *See* Personally identifiable
    information (PII)
PIPEDA. *See* Canadian Personal
    Information Protection and
    Electronic Documents Act
    (PIPEDA)
Plaintext, 56, 57
Plan information, in security plan,
    35f, 36, 38
Platform as a Service
    (PaaS), 17, 115

Policy decomposition, 96, 97f
Post-deployment/release testing, 26
Power, Richard, 10
Privacy, 112–113
Privacy requirements, 93
Privacy Rights Clearinghouse, 20
Privileged and critical operations,
    106–107
Proactive (safeguards) security
    control, 25–26
Productivity of project, 80
Project information, in security
    plan, 35, 35f, 36
Psychological acceptability, 95
Psychological acceptability design
    principle, 65

R

RAD. *See* Rapid application
    development (RAD)
Rainbow table, 57
Rapid application development
    (RAD), 123
RASQ. *See* Relative attack surface
    quotient (RASQ)
Reactive (countermeasures) security
    control, 25
"Recommended Security Controls
    for Federal Information
    Systems and Organizations"
    (NIST), 41–42
Recoverability, 88
Referential integrity, 61
RefRef, 24
Regulations and compliance,
    externally imposed
    security requirements
    and, 90–91
Relative attack surface quotient
    (RASQ), 28
Reliability, 88
Repudiation attacks, 85t

Requirements phase, in building
    security, 26
Resiliency, 88
"Return on Investment" (ROI), 19,
    25, 75, 109
Return on security investment
    (ROSI), 19
RIA. *See* Rich Internet Applications
    (RIA)
Rice, David, 21
Rich Internet Applications (RIA),
    122
Risk and reward, in balancing
    scale, 77–80
"Risk of Incarceration", 109
Rizzo, Juliano, 12
ROI. *See* "Return on Investment"
    (ROI)
Role-and resource-based access
    control mechanisms, 106
Rootkits, 40
ROSI. *See* Return on security
    investment (ROSI)
RSA, 21
Russian posters, 55, 55f

S

SaaS. *See* Software as a Service
    (SaaS)
Salgado, Jr., Carlos Felipe, 10
Salt, 57
SAML. *See* Security Assertion
    Markup Language (SAML)
Sanitization of input, 62
Sarbanes-Oxley Act (SOX), 90
Sarbanes–Oxley (SOX), 40
Savage, Adam, 3
Sbarge, Eric, 81
Schaefer, Joe, 80, 81
Schedule, 79
SC Magazine, 126
Scope of project, 79

SDLC. *See* Security Development
Life Cycle (SDLC);
Software development
life cycle (SDLC); System
Development Life Cycle
(SDLC)
Secure Sockets Layer (SSL), 3, 4,
8–12, 9f, 56
Secure software, 6
Security
silence and, 87–88
software development and,
106–107, 116f
Security Assertion Markup
Language (SAML), 93
Security breach, 20
Security building
elements for, 24–27
need for, 20–24
value-add, 27–28
Security controls
in building security, 25
in security plan, 34, 35f, 36, 37,
37f
Security Development Life Cycle
(SDLC), 26f
Security landscape, 21–22
Security Lingo, 77
Security management interfaces
(SMIs), 67, 68f
Security misconfiguration, 84t
"Security Myths", 14, 15
Security objectives identification, in
security plan development,
39
"Security of Cloud Computing
Provider", 17
Security plan
benefits of, 42–44
overview of, 35–38, 35f
Security plan development, 38–42,
39f
Security professional, 4

Security Quality Requirements
Engineering (SQUARE), 97,
98f
Security requirements, in security
plan, 35, 35f, 36
Security-savvy people, 130–131
Security teams, boardroom
objectives and, 75–77,
76t
Security vs. Functionality, 78
Service Oriented Architectures
(SOA), 93
Service providers, security and,
16–17
Session attacks, 83t
Session hijacking, 83t
Session replay, 83t
Smak. *See* Salgado, Jr., Carlos
Felipe
SMART. *See* Specific, Measurable,
Achievable, Relevant, and
Timely (SMART)
Smart Grid, 93
Smart security objectives, 39
SMIs. *See* Security management
interfaces (SMIs)
Smith, Adam, 18
SOA. *See* Service Oriented
Architectures (SOA)
Social engineering, 85t
Software. *See also* Software,
highly secure; Software
development; Software
security requirements
assurance capability of, 21
insecure, 21
mapped, 44–46
secure, 82, 130–131
Software, highly secure,
133–134
business value and, 18–20
compromising, 15–16
firewall and, 3, 4–8

Internet and accessing, 14–15
introduction, 2–3
intrusion detection systems/
    intrusion prevention
    systems and, 12–14
qualities of, 134f
service providers and, 16–17
software development and,
    104–105
software not accessible from
    Internet, 14–15
SSL and, 8–12
traits of, 28–29
Software adaptability, 120, 122–131
Software as a Service (SaaS), 17,
    114, 115, 122
Software assurance, 3R's of, 27–28,
    27f
Software development
    highly secured software and,
        104–105
    legalities in, 111–115
    secure, stakeholders of, 116f
    stakeholders requirements,
        105–110
Software development life cycle
    (SDLC), 2, 4
Software development team, 110
Software functionality, 44
Software security requirements, 89
    Requirements to retirement,
        99–100
    techniques to, 95–99, 97f, 98f
    traceability of, 99
    types of, 89–94, 90f
Sony, 21, 22, 23f, 24, 111
Sony PlayStation Network,
    2011, 53
SOX. *See* Sarbanes-Oxley Act (SOX);
    Sarbanes–Oxley (SOX)
Specific, Measurable, Achievable,
    Relevant, and Timely
    (SMART), 39

Spoofing, 83t
SP 800 series (NIST), 92
Spyware, 40
SQL Injection, 12
SQL injection attack, 62
SQL slammer worm, 53
SQUARE. *See* Security Quality
    Requirements Engineering
    (SQUARE)
SSL. *See* Secure Sockets Layer (SSL)
sslsniff, 10
sslstrip, 10
Stance training, 81
State Bill 1386, 91
Subject/object modeling process,
    96, 97f
Supergroup, 14, 15
Swiss Federal Data Protection and
    Information Commissioner
    (FDPIC), 112
Symmetric key cryptography, 56
Syntactic bugs, 110
System Development Life Cycle
    (SDLC), 92

T

Talent, software adaptability and,
    127–131
TaoSecurity blog, 20
Technical controls, 37–38, 41
Technology, software adaptability
    and, 122–125
Termination access control, 67
Testing phase, in building security,
    26
"The Cybercrime Service Economy",
    22
"The Peaceful Dragon — The Four
    Right Reasons for Stance
    Training" (Sbarge), 81
Threat agents, 12
Threats

balancing with controls,
83–84t
controls and, 80–82
controls protecting against,
83t
disclosure, 55
external *vs.* internal, 15
identifying, 40, 41f
insider, 14
protecting applications against, 12
real, 12
software adaptability and,
125–127
Threat signatures, 12
T.J. Maxx, 53
TLS. *See* Transport Layer Security
(TLS)
"Top Threats to Cloud Computing"
(Cloud Security Alliance), 115
Transport layer protection,
insufficient, 84t
Transport Layer Security (TLS), 56
Triple Constraints, 78
Trojans, 40
Truman, Harry, 17
Tzu, Sun, 40

U

UDDI. *See* Universal Description,
Discovery and Integration
(UDDI)
Unhandled exceptions, 85t

Universal Description, Discovery
and Integration (UDDI), 93
Unvalidated redirects and forwards,
85t

V

Validation of input, 62
Value, in security, 19–20
Vendors, 114–115
Verbose error messages, 85t
Visualization (plotting) of the log, 14

W

Web application, 9
Web server, SSL and, 9
Web Services Security, 93
WikiLeaks, 24
Wired, 108
World War II American poster,
54, 55f
Writing Secure Code (Howard), 108

X

XACML. *See* eXtensible Access
Control Markup Language
(XACML)
XCP. *See* Extended Copy Protection
(XCP)
XSS attacks. *See* Cross-Site Scripting
(XSS) attacks

Milton Keynes UK
Ingram Content Group UK Ltd.
UKHW031133141024
449569UK00006B/212